5 LAWS OF LIFE

Dr. Maxwell Shimba

TABLE OF CONTENTS

INTRODUCTION

Understanding Life's Laws

Life is a complex journey, marked by myriad experiences, lessons, and moments of growth. Throughout this journey, there are certain principles that, when understood and applied, can significantly enhance our existence. These principles, or "laws," serve as guiding beacons, helping us navigate the uncertainties of life with clarity and purpose. This book aims to explore five fundamental laws of life, delving into their meanings, applications, and the profound impact they can have on our daily lives.

The Need for Guiding Principles

In our modern world, life moves at an unprecedented pace. We are constantly bombarded with information, choices, and challenges, making it easy to feel overwhelmed and lost. Amidst this chaos, having a set of guiding principles can provide a sense of direction and stability. Just as natural laws govern the physical world, these five laws of life can help us understand and manage the complexities of our personal and social existence.

The Five Laws of Life

The laws we will explore in this book are not arbitrary rules imposed from the outside but universal principles that resonate deeply with the human experience. They have been observed and articulated by thinkers, philosophers, and spiritual leaders throughout history. These laws are:

1. The Law of Attraction: The idea that our thoughts and emotions shape our reality.

2. The Law of Cause and Effect: The understanding that every action has a consequence.

3. The Law of Growth: The recognition that change and development are fundamental aspects of life.

4. The Law of Responsibility: The principle that we are accountable for our actions and their outcomes.

5. The Law of Connection: The awareness of the interconnectedness of all life and the importance of relationships.

The Purpose of This Book

This book aims to provide a comprehensive understanding of these five laws and offer practical insights into how they can be applied to enhance our daily lives. By delving into each law, we will uncover its core principles, explore real-life examples, and present actionable strategies for integrating these laws into our personal and professional lives.

A Journey of Self-Discovery

Embarking on this exploration is not just about acquiring knowledge; it is about embarking on a journey of self-discovery and transformation. As we delve into these laws, we will be encouraged to reflect on our own lives, examine our beliefs and behaviors, and make conscious choices that align with these universal principles.

The Structure of This Book

Each chapter of this book is dedicated to one of the five laws. We will start by defining and explaining each law, then move on to practical applications and real-life examples. This structure is designed to provide a balanced blend of theory and practice, ensuring that readers not only understand the laws conceptually but also know how to implement them in their lives.

1. Chapter 1: The Law of Attraction – We will explore how our thoughts and feelings influence our reality and how to harness this power to create the life we desire.

2. Chapter 2: The Law of Cause and Effect – We will delve into the ethical and practical implications of this law, emphasizing the importance of conscious actions and decisions.

3. Chapter 3: The Law of Growth – We will examine the necessity of embracing change and striving for continuous self-improvement.

4. Chapter 4: The Law of Responsibility – We will discuss the significance of taking ownership of our lives and the empowerment that comes from recognizing our role in shaping our destiny.

5. Chapter 5: The Law of Connection – We will highlight the importance of relationships and community, exploring how our interconnectedness enriches our lives.

Why These Laws Matter

Understanding and applying these laws can lead to a more fulfilled and meaningful life. They offer a framework for making sense of our experiences and provide tools for overcoming challenges and achieving our goals. By aligning ourselves with these principles, we can create a life that is not only successful but also deeply satisfying and aligned with our true nature.

Moving Forward

As we embark on this journey together, I encourage you to keep an open mind and a reflective heart. These laws are not just abstract concepts but living truths that can transform your life. By engaging with the ideas and practices presented in this book, you will be taking the first steps toward a more enlightened and empowered existence.

Let us begin this journey of exploration and growth, discovering the profound wisdom and transformative power of the five laws of life.

DR. MAXWELL SHIMBA

CHAPTER 01

THE LAW OF ATTRACTION

The Power of Thought

The Law of Attraction posits that our thoughts and feelings attract corresponding experiences and outcomes. Essentially, what we focus on, we draw into our lives. This chapter explores the mechanics of this law, illustrating how positive thinking, visualization, and emotional alignment can create a reality that mirrors our deepest desires.

Understanding the Power of Thought

Thoughts are powerful forces that shape our reality. They are the seeds from which our experiences grow. Positive, constructive thoughts can lead to fulfilling and joyful experiences, while negative, destructive thoughts can lead to hardship and disappointment. The key to harnessing the Law of Attraction lies in understanding how our thoughts influence our lives and learning to control and direct them toward our goals.

The Science Behind Thought

Modern neuroscience has shown that our brains are incredibly malleable, a characteristic known as neuroplasticity. This means that our thoughts can actually change the structure and function of our brains. Positive thoughts can create new neural pathways that enhance our ability to experience happiness, success, and well-being. Conversely, negative thoughts can reinforce neural pathways associated with stress, anxiety, and depression.

The Thought-Emotion Connection

Thoughts and emotions are deeply interconnected. A thought can trigger an emotional response, and emotions can influence the types of thoughts we have. This interplay creates a feedback loop that can either propel us toward our goals or hinder our progress. By becoming aware of this connection, we can begin to consciously cultivate thoughts that evoke positive emotions and, in turn, attract positive experiences.

Visualization Techniques

One of the most effective ways to harness the power of thought is through visualization. Visualization involves creating a mental image of a desired outcome, allowing us to experience the feelings associated with achieving that outcome as if it has already happened. This technique helps align our thoughts and emotions with our goals, making it more likely that we will attract the desired results.

Steps for Effective Visualization:

1. Set a Clear Intention: Define what you want to achieve with clarity and specificity.

2. Create a Vivid Mental Image: Close your eyes and picture your desired outcome in as much detail as possible.

3. Engage Your Senses: Imagine what you would see, hear, smell, taste, and feel if your goal were already accomplished.

4. Feel the Emotions: Allow yourself to feel the emotions associated with achieving your goal, such as joy, gratitude, and excitement.

5. Repeat Regularly: Practice visualization daily to reinforce your intention and strengthen your emotional connection to your goal.

Affirmations: Reprogramming the Mind

Affirmations are positive statements that can help reprogram our subconscious mind by replacing negative, limiting beliefs with empowering ones. By repeating affirmations regularly, we can cultivate a mindset that supports our goals and attracts positive experiences.

Creating Effective Affirmations:

1. Use the Present Tense: Phrase your affirmations as if they are already true. For example, "I am confident and successful."

2. Keep It Positive: Focus on what you want to achieve, not what you want to avoid. For example, say "I am healthy and vibrant" instead of "I don't want to be sick."

3. Be Specific: Tailor your affirmations to your specific goals and desires.

4. Repeat Consistently: Practice your affirmations daily, preferably in the morning and before bed.

Cultivating a Positive Mindset

A positive mindset is essential for harnessing the power of thought. This involves shifting our focus from negative to positive aspects of our lives and developing habits that support a positive outlook.

Strategies for Cultivating a Positive Mindset:

1. Gratitude Practice: Regularly reflect on the things you are grateful for to shift your focus to the positive aspects of your life.

2. Mindfulness Meditation: Practice mindfulness to become more aware of your thoughts and learn to let go of negative thinking patterns.

3. Surround Yourself with Positivity: Spend time with positive people, engage in uplifting activities, and consume positive content.

4. Challenge Negative Thoughts: When negative thoughts arise, question their validity and replace them with positive alternatives.

The Impact of Environment

Our environment plays a significant role in shaping our thoughts and emotions. By creating a positive environment, we can support our efforts to harness the power of thought.

Creating a Positive Environment:

1. Declutter: Remove physical and mental clutter to create a space that promotes clarity and focus.

2. Incorporate Positive Symbols: Surround yourself with objects and images that inspire and uplift you.

3. Foster Positive Relationships: Build and maintain relationships with people who support and encourage your growth.

Real-Life Examples

Many successful individuals have harnessed the power of thought to achieve their goals. By studying their stories, we can gain insights into how to apply the Law of Attraction in our own lives.

Example 1: Oprah Winfrey

Oprah Winfrey, a media mogul and philanthropist, attributes much of her success to the power of positive thinking and visualization. Despite facing numerous challenges and setbacks, she consistently visualized her goals and maintained a positive mindset, ultimately achieving extraordinary success.

Example 2: Jim Carrey

Actor and comedian Jim Carrey famously used visualization to achieve his dream of becoming a successful actor. He wrote himself a check for $10 million for "acting services rendered" and carried it in his wallet for years. He visualized himself receiving this amount for a role, and in 1994, he was offered a role in "Dumb and Dumber" for $10 million.

The power of thought is a fundamental aspect of the Law of Attraction. By understanding and harnessing this power, we can shape our reality and attract the experiences and outcomes we desire. Through visualization, affirmations, cultivating a positive mindset, and creating a supportive environment, we can align our thoughts and emotions with our goals, making our dreams a reality. As we move forward in this book, we will explore additional laws that complement the power of thought, further enhancing our ability to create a fulfilling and purposeful life.

Visualization Techniques: Detailed Methods for Visualizing Goals and Dreams

Visualization is a powerful tool that helps translate our dreams and goals into reality. It involves creating vivid mental images of desired outcomes, allowing us to experience the emotions associated with achieving these goals. By engaging our senses and emotions in the visualization process, we align our thoughts with our intentions, making it more likely for us to attract the desired results. This chapter will delve into various visualization techniques, offering detailed methods to effectively visualize goals and dreams.

Understanding Visualization

Visualization is more than just daydreaming; it is a focused and deliberate practice of imagining future events. This technique taps into the brain's ability to simulate experiences and emotions, helping us prepare for and manifest our desired outcomes. Scientific research has shown that the brain cannot distinguish between real and vividly imagined experiences, making visualization a potent tool for personal development and goal achievement.

The Science Behind Visualization

The brain's neuroplasticity allows it to form new neural pathways based on our thoughts and experiences. When we visualize a desired outcome, we activate the same neural networks that would be used if we were actually experiencing that outcome. This primes our brain for success, enhancing our motivation, focus, and resilience.

Steps for Effective Visualization

To harness the full power of visualization, it is essential to follow a structured approach. The following steps provide a comprehensive guide to effective visualization:

1. Set a Clear Intention:

- Define your goal with clarity and specificity. What exactly do you want to achieve? The more precise you are, the more effective your visualization will be.

- Write down your goal in a positive and present-tense statement, such as "I am successfully leading my team to complete the project on time."

2. Find a Quiet Space:

- Choose a quiet and comfortable place where you won't be disturbed. This helps you focus and immerse yourself in the visualization process.

3. Relax and Center Yourself:

- Take a few deep breaths to relax your body and mind. Close your eyes and let go of any tension or distractions.

- Use relaxation techniques such as progressive muscle relaxation or deep breathing exercises to achieve a calm state.

4. Create a Vivid Mental Image:

- Picture your desired outcome in as much detail as possible. Imagine the scene as if it is happening right now.

- Include specific elements such as the environment, people involved, and any relevant objects. The more detailed your mental image, the more powerful the visualization.

5. Engage All Your Senses:

- Imagine what you would see, hear, smell, taste, and feel if your goal were already accomplished.

- For example, if you are visualizing a successful presentation, imagine the sight of the audience, the sound of applause, the feeling of confidence, and even the smell of the room.

6. Feel the Emotions:

- Allow yourself to experience the emotions associated with achieving your goal. Feel the joy, excitement, gratitude, and satisfaction as if your dream has already come true.

- Emotional engagement is crucial as it strengthens the neural connections related to your goal, making the visualization more effective.

7. Repeat Regularly:

- Practice visualization daily, preferably in the morning and before bed. Consistency reinforces your intention and strengthens your emotional connection to your goal.

- Spend at least 10-15 minutes each session to fully immerse yourself in the visualization process.

Advanced Visualization Techniques

Once you have mastered the basic steps, you can enhance your visualization practice with advanced techniques:

1. Vision Board:

- Create a vision board by compiling images, quotes, and symbols that represent your goals. Place it in a location where you will see it daily.

- Regularly look at your vision board and visualize yourself achieving the goals depicted on it.

2. Visualization Scripts:

- Write a detailed script describing your desired outcome as if it has already happened. Include sensory details and emotions.

- Read your script aloud during your visualization sessions, allowing yourself to fully experience the scenario.

3. Guided Visualization:

- Use guided visualization recordings or apps that lead you through the visualization process. These can be particularly helpful for beginners or when focusing on specific goals.

- Follow the instructions and immerse yourself in the guided experience.

4. Dynamic Visualization:

- Combine visualization with physical movements. For example, if you are visualizing a successful sports performance, mimic the actions and movements involved.

- This technique enhances the mind-body connection and reinforces the neural pathways related to your goal.

Overcoming Common Challenges

Visualization can be challenging, especially for beginners. Here are some common obstacles and tips to overcome them:

1. Lack of Clarity:

- If you struggle to visualize details, start with a general image and gradually add more specifics over time.

- Practice focusing on one aspect of your goal at a time, such as the environment or emotions, before combining all elements.

2. Distractions:

- Create a dedicated space for visualization that is free from distractions. Use earplugs or calming background music to block out noise.

- Set a timer for your visualization sessions to help you stay focused and committed.

3. Negative Thoughts:

- Acknowledge any negative thoughts that arise during visualization and gently redirect your focus to positive aspects.

- Use affirmations to counteract negative thinking and reinforce positive beliefs.

4. Impatience:

- Remember that visualization is a skill that improves with practice. Be patient and consistent, trusting the process.

- Celebrate small successes and progress along the way to stay motivated.

Real-Life Examples of Successful Visualization

Many successful individuals attribute their achievements to the practice of visualization. Here are a few inspiring examples:

Example 1: Michael Phelps

Olympic swimmer Michael Phelps used visualization to prepare for his races. He would mentally rehearse every aspect of his performance, from the start to the finish, including how he would handle unexpected challenges. This practice helped him achieve unprecedented success, winning 23 gold medals.

Example 2: Arnold Schwarzenegger

Actor and former governor Arnold Schwarzenegger used visualization to achieve his bodybuilding and acting goals. He would visualize himself holding the Mr. Olympia trophy and starring in blockbuster movies. His focused visualization practice played a significant role in his success.

Example 3: Oprah Winfrey

Media mogul Oprah Winfrey has spoken about the power of visualization in her career. She would visualize herself achieving her dreams, such as hosting a successful talk show and building a media empire. Her dedication to visualization helped her overcome challenges and reach extraordinary heights.

Visualization is a transformative practice that can help you achieve your goals and create the life you desire. By following the detailed methods outlined in this chapter, you can harness the power of visualization to align your thoughts, emotions, and actions with your intentions. Remember to practice regularly, engage your senses, and immerse yourself in the experience. With dedication and consistency, visualization can become a powerful tool for manifesting your dreams and realizing your fullest potential. As we continue exploring the Law of Attraction in this book, we will uncover additional techniques and principles to further enhance your journey toward a fulfilling and purposeful life.

Affirmations: Crafting and Using Affirmations to Reinforce Positive Beliefs

Affirmations are powerful statements that can help reprogram our subconscious mind by replacing negative, limiting beliefs with positive, empowering ones. By consistently repeating affirmations, we can cultivate a mindset that supports our goals and attracts positive experiences. This chapter delves into the art of crafting effective affirmations and provides practical guidance on how to use them to reinforce positive beliefs.

Understanding Affirmations

Affirmations are positive statements that describe a desired situation or goal in its completed state. They are a tool to help you believe in the potential of your actions and to remind you of your capabilities. By repeating affirmations regularly, you can begin to change your thought patterns and align your beliefs with your goals.

The Science Behind Affirmations

The brain has the ability to form new neural pathways based on our thoughts and repeated experiences. Affirmations work by creating these new pathways, helping us shift from negative thinking patterns to positive ones. When we repeat affirmations, we engage in a process called neuroplasticity, which allows our brain to adapt and change. This can lead to improved mental health, increased motivation, and greater resilience in the face of challenges.

Crafting Effective Affirmations

To create powerful and effective affirmations, it is important to follow certain guidelines. Here are the key elements of crafting affirmations that resonate and bring about positive change:

1. Use the Present Tense:

   - Phrase your affirmations as if they are already true. This helps your subconscious mind accept them as reality.

- Example: "I am confident and successful" instead of "I will be confident and successful."

2. Be Positive:

- Focus on what you want to achieve, not what you want to avoid. Frame your affirmations in a positive manner to reinforce constructive beliefs.

- Example: "I am healthy and energetic" instead of "I don't want to be tired and sick."

3. Be Specific:

- Tailor your affirmations to your specific goals and desires. The more detailed and precise, the more effective they will be.

- Example: "I am earning $5,000 per month through my creative writing" instead of "I want to make more money."

4. Include Emotion:

- Infuse your affirmations with emotions that you would feel when achieving your goals. This strengthens the connection between your thoughts and your desires.

- Example: "I am joyfully receiving love and support from my friends and family" instead of "I want to be loved."

5. Keep It Believable:

- Make sure your affirmations are realistic and believable. If your subconscious mind rejects them as unrealistic, they will not be effective.

- Example: "I am progressing towards a healthier lifestyle" instead of "I am the healthiest person in the world."

Examples of Affirmations

Here are some examples of affirmations for different areas of life:

Health:

- "I am vibrant, healthy, and full of energy."

- "My body is strong and capable of healing itself."

Career:

- "I am excelling in my career and attracting new opportunities for growth."

- "I am a valuable and respected member of my team."

Relationships:

- "I am surrounded by loving and supportive relationships."

- "I attract positive and kind people into my life."

Self-Confidence:

- "I am confident in my abilities and trust myself to make the right decisions."

- "I believe in myself and my potential to achieve great things."

Financial Abundance:

- "I am attracting financial abundance and prosperity into my life."

- "Money flows to me easily and effortlessly."

Using Affirmations Effectively

To maximize the effectiveness of your affirmations, it is important to incorporate them into your daily routine and practice them consistently. Here are some strategies for using affirmations effectively:

1. Daily Practice:

- Set aside specific times each day to repeat your affirmations. Morning and evening are ideal times to reinforce positive beliefs.

- Spend a few minutes each session, repeating each affirmation slowly and with conviction.

2. Visualization:

- Combine affirmations with visualization to enhance their power. As you repeat your affirmations, visualize yourself achieving your goals and experiencing the associated emotions.

- Engage all your senses in the visualization process to make it more vivid and impactful.

3. Written Affirmations:

- Write your affirmations in a journal or on index cards. Writing helps reinforce the message and makes it more tangible.

- Review and update your written affirmations regularly to keep them aligned with your current goals and desires.

4. Affirmation Cards:

- Create affirmation cards that you can carry with you or place in prominent locations. These serve as constant reminders of your positive beliefs.

- Place them on your bathroom mirror, in your car, or at your workstation to keep your affirmations top of mind.

5. Affirmation Apps:

- Use affirmation apps or digital tools that send you reminders throughout the day. These can help you stay consistent with your practice and reinforce positive beliefs.

- Set notifications to receive your affirmations at regular intervals, keeping your mind focused on your goals.

6. Mirror Work:

- Stand in front of a mirror and repeat your affirmations while looking into your own eyes. This practice can enhance self-acceptance and confidence.

- Speak your affirmations with enthusiasm and conviction, as if you are speaking to a dear friend.

7. Affirmation Meditation:

- Incorporate affirmations into your meditation practice. Begin your meditation with a few minutes of repeating your affirmations to set a positive tone.

- Focus on the words and the feelings they evoke, allowing them to resonate deeply within you.

Real-Life Examples of Affirmation Success

Many individuals have achieved remarkable success by incorporating affirmations into their daily lives. Here are a few inspiring examples:

Example 1: Louise Hay

Louise Hay, a renowned author and motivational speaker, is a pioneer in the use of affirmations for healing and personal growth. She overcame a traumatic past and health challenges by using affirmations to change her thought patterns and beliefs. Her book, "You Can Heal Your Life," has helped millions of people transform their lives through the power of affirmations.

Example 2: Will Smith

Actor and musician Will Smith has spoken about the importance of positive thinking and affirmations in his career. He uses affirmations to stay focused on his goals and maintain a positive mindset. His belief in the power of his words and thoughts has played a significant role in his success.

Example 3: Jim Carrey

Actor Jim Carrey famously used affirmations to manifest his career success. He wrote himself a check for $10 million for "acting services rendered" and kept it in his wallet. He visualized receiving this amount for a film role, and a few years later, he was offered a $10 million role in "Dumb and Dumber."

Affirmations are a powerful tool for transforming your thoughts and beliefs, aligning them with your goals, and attracting positive experiences. By crafting effective affirmations and incorporating them into your daily routine, you can reprogram your subconscious mind and cultivate a mindset that supports your success and well-being. Remember to practice consistently, engage your emotions, and believe in the power of your affirmations. As you continue your journey through the Law of Attraction, affirmations will serve as a cornerstone for creating a fulfilling and purposeful life.

Mindfulness Practices: Techniques for Maintaining a Positive Focus in Daily Life

Mindfulness is the practice of being fully present and engaged in the current moment. It involves paying attention to our thoughts, feelings, and surroundings without judgment. By cultivating mindfulness, we can maintain a positive focus in our daily lives, reduce stress, and enhance our overall well-being. This chapter explores various mindfulness techniques and provides practical guidance on incorporating them into your routine to support the Law of Attraction.

Understanding Mindfulness

Mindfulness is rooted in ancient meditation practices but has gained significant attention in modern psychology and wellness. It involves bringing awareness to the present moment, observing thoughts and emotions without getting caught up in them, and fostering an attitude of acceptance. By practicing mindfulness, we can break free from negative thought patterns and focus on positive experiences and intentions.

The Benefits of Mindfulness

The benefits of mindfulness are well-documented and include:

1. Reduced Stress: Mindfulness helps lower stress levels by promoting relaxation and reducing the body's stress response.

2. Improved Emotional Regulation: It enhances our ability to manage emotions and respond to situations calmly and thoughtfully.

3. Enhanced Focus and Concentration: Mindfulness sharpens our attention, making it easier to concentrate on tasks and achieve our goals.

4. Greater Self-Awareness: It increases our awareness of thoughts, feelings, and behaviors, enabling us to make more conscious choices.

5. Better Mental Health: Regular mindfulness practice can reduce symptoms of anxiety and depression, promoting overall mental well-being.

Techniques for Practicing Mindfulness

There are several mindfulness techniques that can help you maintain a positive focus in daily life. Here are some effective practices to consider:

1. Mindful Breathing:

- Description: Focus your attention on your breath. Observe the sensation of the air entering and leaving your nostrils or the rise and fall of your chest or abdomen.

- Practice: Set aside a few minutes each day to practice mindful breathing. Whenever you notice your mind wandering, gently bring your attention back to your breath.

2. Body Scan Meditation:

- Description: Perform a mental scan of your body, paying attention to any sensations, tension, or areas of relaxation.

- Practice: Lie down or sit comfortably. Starting from your toes and moving up to your head, focus on each part of your body, noticing any physical sensations without judgment.

3. Mindful Eating:

- Description: Bring full awareness to the experience of eating. Notice the colors, textures, flavors, and smells of your food.

- Practice: Eat slowly and deliberately, savoring each bite. Pay attention to the sensations in your mouth and the act of chewing and swallowing.

4. Mindful Walking:

- Description: Walk slowly and mindfully, paying attention to the sensations of movement and the environment around you.

- Practice: Take a walk in a quiet place. Focus on the feeling of your feet touching the ground, the movement of your legs, and the sights and sounds around you.

5. Loving-Kindness Meditation:

- Description: Cultivate feelings of compassion and kindness towards yourself and others.

- Practice: Sit comfortably and silently repeat phrases such as "May I be happy, may I be healthy, may I be safe." Gradually extend these wishes to others, including loved ones, acquaintances, and even those with whom you have difficulties.

6. Mindful Journaling:

- Description: Reflect on your thoughts and emotions by writing them down without judgment.

- Practice: Set aside time each day to journal. Write about your experiences, feelings, and any insights you have gained. Use this practice to cultivate self-awareness and positive thinking.

Incorporating Mindfulness into Daily Life

To maintain a positive focus, it is important to integrate mindfulness into your daily routine. Here are some strategies to help you make mindfulness a regular part of your life:

1. Create a Mindfulness Routine:

- Establish a daily schedule for mindfulness practices. Whether it's in the morning, during a break, or before bed, consistency is key.

- Start with short sessions and gradually increase the duration as you become more comfortable.

2. Mindfulness Reminders:

- Use reminders to bring your attention back to the present moment. Set alarms or use mindfulness apps to prompt you to pause and practice mindfulness.

- Place visual reminders, such as sticky notes or images, in your environment to remind you to stay present.

3. Mindful Transitions:

- Use transitions between activities as opportunities for mindfulness. Take a few deep breaths and center yourself before moving from one task to another.

- Practice mindful walking or breathing during short breaks to refresh your mind and body.

4. Mindfulness in Daily Activities:

- Integrate mindfulness into routine tasks such as washing dishes, brushing your teeth, or driving. Focus on the sensations and actions involved in these activities.

- Approach each task with curiosity and attention, turning mundane moments into opportunities for mindfulness.

5. Mindful Communication:

- Practice active listening and present-moment awareness during conversations. Pay attention to the speaker without planning your response.

- Respond thoughtfully and with empathy, fostering deeper and more meaningful connections.

Overcoming Challenges in Mindfulness Practice

Mindfulness practice can come with challenges, especially in the beginning. Here are some common obstacles and tips to overcome them:

1. Restlessness:

- If you find it difficult to sit still, start with shorter mindfulness sessions and gradually increase the duration.

- Incorporate movement-based practices such as mindful walking or yoga.

2. Distracting Thoughts:

- It is natural for thoughts to arise during mindfulness practice. Acknowledge them without judgment and gently bring your focus back to the present moment.

- Use your breath as an anchor to help refocus your attention.

3. Impatience:

- Mindfulness is a skill that develops over time. Be patient with yourself and recognize that progress may be gradual.

- Celebrate small successes and improvements in your mindfulness practice.

4. Self-Criticism:

- Avoid judging yourself for getting distracted or finding mindfulness difficult. Approach your practice with self-compassion and understanding.

- Remember that mindfulness is about observation without judgment, including self-observation.

Real-Life Examples of Mindfulness Success

Many individuals have experienced profound benefits from incorporating mindfulness into their lives. Here are a few inspiring examples:

Example 1: Jon Kabat-Zinn

Jon Kabat-Zinn, a pioneer in mindfulness-based stress reduction (MBSR), has helped thousands of people improve their mental and physical health through mindfulness. His work has demonstrated the effectiveness of mindfulness in reducing stress, anxiety, and chronic pain.

Example 2: LeBron James

NBA superstar LeBron James practices mindfulness to enhance his focus and performance on the court. He uses techniques such as meditation and visualization to maintain a positive mindset and manage the pressures of professional sports.

Example 3: Arianna Huffington

Arianna Huffington, founder of The Huffington Post, incorporates mindfulness into her daily routine to manage stress and maintain work-life balance. She advocates for the importance of mindfulness in achieving success and well-being.

Mindfulness is a powerful practice for maintaining a positive focus and enhancing overall well-being. By incorporating mindfulness techniques into your daily life, you can cultivate greater self-awareness, reduce stress, and align your thoughts with your goals. Remember to practice consistently, approach mindfulness with curiosity and compassion, and be patient with yourself as you develop this valuable skill. As you continue exploring the Law of Attraction, mindfulness will serve as a foundational practice for creating a fulfilling and purposeful life.

Real-Life Examples: Stories of Individuals Who Have Successfully Harnessed the Law of Attraction

The Law of Attraction has been a guiding principle for many successful individuals across various fields. By understanding and applying this law, they have transformed their thoughts and emotions into powerful tools for achieving their goals. In this chapter, we explore real-life stories of people who have effectively harnessed the Law of Attraction, offering inspiration and practical insights for your own journey.

Example 1: Oprah Winfrey

Background:

Oprah Winfrey, a media mogul, philanthropist, and one of the most influential women in the world, has often spoken about the role of the Law of Attraction in her life. Growing up in poverty and facing numerous challenges, Oprah used the power of positive thinking and visualization to rise above her circumstances.

Application of the Law of Attraction:

Oprah consistently visualized herself achieving greatness. She would dream about being a successful television host and having a platform to help others. She used affirmations and maintained a positive mindset, despite the obstacles she faced.

Outcome:

Oprah's unwavering belief in her dreams and her practice of positive thinking led to her becoming one of the most successful media personalities in history. She hosted "The Oprah Winfrey Show," which became the highest-rated television talk show, and she built a media empire. Oprah's story demonstrates how the Law of Attraction can help transform adversity into extraordinary success.

Practical Insights:

- Maintain a clear vision of your goals, even in the face of challenges.

- Use affirmations to reinforce positive beliefs.

- Stay focused on your dreams and remain resilient.

Example 2: Jim Carrey

Background:

Jim Carrey, a renowned actor and comedian, is another example of someone who has successfully used the Law of Attraction. Before achieving fame, Carrey faced financial struggles and numerous rejections in his acting career.

Application of the Law of Attraction:

Carrey used visualization and affirmations to manifest his dreams. He famously wrote himself a check for $10 million for "acting services rendered" and dated it five years in the future. He carried this check in his wallet and visualized himself receiving that amount for a film role.

Outcome:

In 1994, Carrey's visualization came to fruition when he was cast in the film "Dumb and Dumber" and received a $10 million paycheck. His belief in the Law of Attraction and his practice of visualization played a significant role in his rise to stardom.

Practical Insights:

- Create tangible symbols of your goals, such as writing yourself a check or creating a vision board.

- Regularly visualize your success and feel the emotions associated with achieving your dreams.

- Maintain a positive and persistent attitude, even during challenging times.

Example 3: Arnold Schwarzenegger

Background:

Arnold Schwarzenegger, a bodybuilder, actor, and former governor of California, has attributed much of his success to the Law of Attraction. Born in Austria, Schwarzenegger had a dream of moving to America and becoming a successful bodybuilder and actor.

Application of the Law of Attraction:

Schwarzenegger used visualization to achieve his goals. As a young man, he would visualize himself standing on stage, holding the Mr. Olympia trophy. He also visualized becoming a Hollywood star, despite having no connections in the industry.

Outcome:

Schwarzenegger's dedication to his vision led him to win the Mr. Olympia title seven times and become one of the most famous bodybuilders in history. He then transitioned to acting and starred in blockbuster films such as "The Terminator" and "Predator." His visualization and belief in the Law of Attraction also helped him achieve political success as the governor of California.

Practical Insights:

- Visualize your goals with clarity and detail.

- Consistently reinforce your vision through daily practice.

- Believe in your ability to achieve your dreams, regardless of current circumstances.

Example 4: Sara Blakely

Background:

Sara Blakely, the founder of Spanx, turned a simple idea into a billion-dollar business. Before her success, Blakely faced numerous rejections and financial struggles.

Application of the Law of Attraction:

Blakely used visualization and positive thinking to manifest her business success. She would visualize her products being sold in major department stores and imagine herself as a successful entrepreneur. She also used affirmations to build her confidence and stay motivated.

Outcome:

Blakely's belief in her vision and her application of the Law of Attraction led to Spanx becoming a global brand. She became the youngest self-made female billionaire and continues to inspire entrepreneurs around the world.

Practical Insights:

- Visualize the success of your ideas and projects.

- Use affirmations to boost your confidence and motivation.

- Stay persistent and resilient, even in the face of rejection.

Example 5: Will Smith

Background:

Will Smith, a successful actor, producer, and musician, has often spoken about the power of positive thinking and the Law of Attraction in his career. Smith faced early challenges, including financial difficulties and career setbacks.

Application of the Law of Attraction:

Smith used visualization and positive affirmations to shape his career. He visualized himself achieving success in the entertainment industry and consistently maintained a positive mindset. Smith believes that our thoughts and words have a powerful impact on our reality.

Outcome:

Smith's positive thinking and visualization techniques helped him become one of the most successful actors in Hollywood, starring in blockbuster films such as "Independence Day" and "Men in Black." His career spans music, television, and film, demonstrating the effectiveness of the Law of Attraction.

Practical Insights:

- Visualize your success in vivid detail.

- Use positive affirmations to reinforce your beliefs and goals.

- Maintain a positive attitude and stay focused on your vision.

These real-life examples demonstrate the transformative power of the Law of Attraction. By harnessing the power of positive thinking, visualization, and affirmations, these individuals achieved extraordinary success in their respective fields. Their stories offer practical insights and inspiration for anyone looking to apply the Law of Attraction to their own lives. Remember, maintaining a positive focus and believing in your ability to achieve your goals are essential steps in manifesting your dreams and creating a fulfilling life. As you continue exploring the Law of Attraction, let these examples guide and motivate you on your journey to success.

Oprah Winfrey

Background

Oprah Winfrey, a media mogul, philanthropist, and one of the most influential women in the world, has often spoken about the role of the Law of Attraction in her life. Her journey from a challenging childhood to becoming a global icon is a testament to the power of positive thinking and visualization. Growing up in poverty and facing numerous challenges, including abuse and discrimination, Oprah used the power of her mind to rise above her circumstances and achieve extraordinary success.

Early Life and Challenges

Oprah Gail Winfrey was born on January 29, 1954, in Kosciusko, Mississippi. Raised by her grandmother in dire poverty, Oprah experienced hardships that could have easily deterred her from pursuing her dreams. Her grandmother taught her to read before the age of three, and she often recited Bible verses at church, which instilled in her a love for speaking and performing.

At the age of six, Oprah moved to Milwaukee, Wisconsin, to live with her mother. During this time, she faced severe physical and sexual abuse from family members, which profoundly impacted her. Despite these challenges, Oprah excelled in school and won a scholarship to Tennessee State University, where she pursued a degree in Communications.

The Role of the Law of Attraction

Oprah's belief in the Law of Attraction began to take shape as she navigated the early years of her career. She consistently visualized herself achieving greatness and used positive affirmations to maintain her focus and motivation. Oprah understood that her thoughts had the power to shape her reality, and she diligently applied this principle to her life.

1. Visualization and Positive Thinking:

Oprah often spoke about the importance of visualizing success. She would imagine herself hosting a successful television show and having a platform to help others. This clear vision of her future drove her actions and decisions, guiding her toward her goals.

2. Affirmations and Self-Belief:

Oprah used affirmations to reinforce her positive beliefs. She would tell herself, "I am destined for greatness," and "I have the power to create my own destiny." These affirmations helped her build confidence and stay focused on her dreams, even during difficult times.

3. Maintaining a Positive Mindset:

Despite the numerous obstacles she faced, Oprah maintained a positive mindset. She believed that every experience, good or bad, was an opportunity for growth and learning. This outlook allowed her to overcome challenges and continue moving forward.

Achieving Extraordinary Success

Oprah's dedication to the Law of Attraction and her unwavering belief in her dreams led to her achieving extraordinary success. Here are some key milestones in her journey:

1. The Oprah Winfrey Show:

In 1984, Oprah moved to Chicago to host a low-rated morning talk show called "AM Chicago." Within months, the show's ratings skyrocketed, and it was renamed "The Oprah Winfrey Show." The show became the highest-rated television talk show in history, running for 25 years and earning numerous awards.

2. Building a Media Empire:

Oprah leveraged her success on television to build a media empire. She founded Harpo Productions, a multimedia production company, and launched the Oprah Winfrey Network (OWN). Her media ventures expanded her influence and provided a platform for diverse voices and stories.

3. Philanthropy and Advocacy:

Oprah's success enabled her to give back to the community and advocate for various causes. She established the Oprah Winfrey Foundation and the Oprah Winfrey Leadership Academy for Girls in South Africa, among other philanthropic efforts. Her charitable work has impacted countless lives and inspired others to contribute to positive change.

4. Recognition and Awards:

Throughout her career, Oprah has received numerous accolades, including the Presidential Medal of Freedom, honorary degrees from prestigious universities, and recognition as one of the most powerful women in the world by Forbes. Her achievements underscore the impact of her dedication to the Law of Attraction and her belief in the power of positive thinking.

Practical Insights from Oprah's Journey

Oprah's journey offers valuable lessons for anyone looking to apply the Law of Attraction in their own lives. Here are some practical insights:

1. Visualize Your Goals:

Take time each day to visualize your goals with clarity and detail. Imagine yourself achieving your dreams and experiencing the associated emotions. This practice helps align your thoughts and actions with your intentions.

2. Use Affirmations:

Create positive affirmations that reinforce your beliefs and goals. Repeat them daily to build confidence and maintain focus. For example, you might say, "I am capable of achieving my dreams," or "I attract success and abundance into my life."

3. Maintain a Positive Mindset:

Cultivate a positive mindset by focusing on opportunities for growth and learning in every experience. When faced with challenges, remind yourself that setbacks are temporary and can be overcome with perseverance and determination.

4. Surround Yourself with Positivity:

Surround yourself with positive influences, including supportive people, inspiring books, and uplifting environments. This helps reinforce your positive beliefs and keeps you motivated.

5. Take Action:

While positive thinking and visualization are important, they must be coupled with action. Take consistent steps toward your goals, and trust that your efforts will lead to success.

Oprah Winfrey's story is a powerful testament to the transformative power of the Law of Attraction. By visualizing her success, using affirmations, and maintaining a positive mindset, she rose above her challenging circumstances to become one of the most influential women in the world. Her journey offers inspiration and practical insights for anyone seeking to harness the power of positive thinking and achieve their dreams. As you continue exploring the Law of Attraction, let Oprah's story guide and motivate you on your own path to success and fulfillment.

Jim Carrey

Background

Jim Carrey, a renowned actor and comedian, is another example of someone who has successfully used the Law of Attraction to achieve extraordinary success. Before his rise to fame, Carrey faced significant financial struggles and numerous rejections in his acting career. His journey from a challenging upbringing to becoming one of Hollywood's most beloved actors demonstrates the power of positive thinking, visualization, and persistence.

Early Life and Challenges

Jim Carrey was born on January 17, 1962, in Newmarket, Ontario, Canada. Growing up in a low-income family, Carrey experienced hardship from an early age. His father lost his job, forcing the family to live in a van for a period of time. Despite these difficulties, Carrey discovered his talent for comedy and acting at a young age.

During his teenage years, Carrey performed in comedy clubs to help support his family financially. His initial performances were met with mixed reactions, and he faced numerous rejections as he tried to establish himself in the entertainment industry. However, Carrey's unwavering belief in his talent and his ability to make people laugh kept him going.

The Role of the Law of Attraction

Jim Carrey's belief in the Law of Attraction began to take shape as he navigated the early stages of his career. He understood that his thoughts and emotions had the power to influence his reality, and he used visualization and positive affirmations to attract the success he desired.

1. Visualization and Positive Thinking:

Carrey often spoke about the importance of visualizing success. He would imagine himself achieving his goals and experiencing the emotions associated with his dreams. This clear vision of his future guided his actions and decisions.

2. Affirmations and Self-Belief:

Carrey used affirmations to reinforce his positive beliefs. He would tell himself, "I am a successful actor," and "I have the power to achieve my dreams." These affirmations helped him build confidence and stay focused on his goals, even during tough times.

3. Maintaining a Positive Mindset:

Despite facing numerous rejections and financial hardships, Carrey maintained a positive mindset. He believed that every setback was a step closer to his success and that his dreams were within reach.

Achieving Extraordinary Success

Jim Carrey's dedication to the Law of Attraction and his unwavering belief in his dreams led to his achieving extraordinary success. Here are some key milestones in his journey:

1. The $10 Million Check:

One of the most famous examples of Carrey's use of the Law of Attraction is the $10 million check he wrote to himself. In the early 1990s, Carrey wrote a check for $10 million for "acting services rendered" and dated it Thanksgiving 1995. He carried this check in his wallet and visualized receiving this amount for a film role. In 1994, Carrey was cast in the film "Dumb and Dumber" and received a $10 million paycheck, fulfilling his visualization.

2. Breakthrough Roles:

Carrey's persistence and positive thinking led to breakthrough roles in films such as "Ace Ventura: Pet Detective," "The Mask," and "Liar Liar." These films showcased his comedic talent and established him as a leading actor in Hollywood.

3. Expanding His Range:

Beyond comedy, Carrey took on more serious roles in films like "The Truman Show" and "Eternal Sunshine of the Spotless Mind," earning critical acclaim for his performances. His ability to excel in both comedic and dramatic roles demonstrated his versatility as an actor.

4. Philanthropy and Advocacy:

Carrey's success allowed him to give back to the community and advocate for causes he is passionate about. He has been involved in various charitable activities and has used his platform to raise awareness about mental health and other important issues.

5. Recognition and Awards:

Throughout his career, Carrey has received numerous awards and accolades, including Golden Globe Awards for his performances in "The Truman Show" and "Man on the Moon." His achievements underscore the impact of his dedication to the Law of Attraction and his belief in the power of positive thinking.

Practical Insights from Jim Carrey's Journey

Jim Carrey's journey offers valuable lessons for anyone looking to apply the Law of Attraction in their own lives. Here are some practical insights:

1. Visualize Your Goals:

Take time each day to visualize your goals with clarity and detail. Imagine yourself achieving your dreams and experiencing the associated emotions. This practice helps align your thoughts and actions with your intentions.

2. Use Affirmations:

Create positive affirmations that reinforce your beliefs and goals. Repeat them daily to build confidence and maintain focus. For example, you might say, "I am capable of achieving my dreams," or "I attract success and abundance into my life."

3. Maintain a Positive Mindset:

Cultivate a positive mindset by focusing on opportunities for growth and learning in every experience. When faced with challenges, remind yourself that setbacks are temporary and can be overcome with perseverance and determination.

4. Surround Yourself with Positivity:

Surround yourself with positive influences, including supportive people, inspiring books, and uplifting environments. This helps reinforce your positive beliefs and keeps you motivated.

5. Take Action:

While positive thinking and visualization are important, they must be coupled with action. Take consistent steps toward your goals, and trust that your efforts will lead to success.

Jim Carrey's story is a powerful testament to the transformative power of the Law of Attraction. By visualizing his success, using affirmations, and maintaining a positive mindset, he rose above his challenging circumstances to become one of Hollywood's most beloved actors. His journey offers inspiration and practical insights for anyone seeking to harness the power of positive thinking and achieve their dreams. As you continue exploring the Law of Attraction, let Jim Carrey's story guide and motivate you on your own path to success and fulfillment.

Arnold Schwarzenegger

Background

Arnold Schwarzenegger, a bodybuilder, actor, and former governor of California, has attributed much of his success to the Law of Attraction. Born on July 30, 1947, in Thal, Austria, Schwarzenegger had a dream of moving to America and becoming a successful bodybuilder and actor. His journey from a small village in Austria to becoming one of the most recognized personalities in the world is a testament to the power of visualization, positive thinking, and relentless pursuit of one's goals.

Early Life and Challenges

Arnold Schwarzenegger grew up in post-World War II Austria, a time and place marked by scarcity and rebuilding. His family was not wealthy, and his father, a local police chief, had strict expectations for his children. Despite these challenges, Schwarzenegger developed an interest in physical fitness and bodybuilding at a young age.

Inspired by the bodybuilding champion Reg Park, Schwarzenegger set his sights on moving to America, becoming a champion bodybuilder, and breaking into Hollywood. This dream seemed almost impossible given his circumstances, but Schwarzenegger's belief in the Law of Attraction and his unwavering determination set him on a path to extraordinary success.

The Role of the Law of Attraction

Arnold Schwarzenegger's belief in the Law of Attraction played a crucial role in his journey. He used visualization and positive thinking to align his thoughts with his goals, which helped him stay focused and motivated despite numerous obstacles.

1. Visualization and Positive Thinking:

Schwarzenegger was a firm believer in visualization. He would create vivid mental images of himself achieving his goals. For instance, he visualized himself winning bodybuilding competitions, starring in blockbuster movies, and becoming a successful entrepreneur and politician.

2. Affirmations and Self-Belief:

Schwarzenegger used affirmations to reinforce his goals. He would regularly tell himself that he was destined for greatness and capable of achieving his dreams. These affirmations helped him maintain confidence and determination, even when faced with setbacks.

3. Maintaining a Positive Mindset:

Throughout his journey, Schwarzenegger maintained a positive mindset. He viewed challenges as opportunities for growth and learning. This optimistic outlook enabled him to persevere through difficult times and continue working towards his goals.

Achieving Extraordinary Success

Arnold Schwarzenegger's dedication to the Law of Attraction and his unwavering belief in his dreams led to his achieving extraordinary success in multiple fields. Here are some key milestones in his journey:

1. Bodybuilding Champion:

Schwarzenegger's visualization techniques paid off when he became the youngest Mr. Universe at the age of 20. He went on to win the Mr. Olympia title seven times, solidifying his place as one of the greatest bodybuilders in history. His relentless pursuit of excellence in bodybuilding was fueled by his ability to visualize his success and stay focused on his goals.

2. Hollywood Stardom:

After conquering the world of bodybuilding, Schwarzenegger set his sights on Hollywood. Despite having a thick accent and limited acting experience, he visualized himself becoming a successful actor. His breakout role came with "Conan the Barbarian" in 1982, followed by iconic roles in films such as "The Terminator," "Predator," and "Total Recall." His success in Hollywood was a direct result of his ability to turn his dreams into reality through the power of visualization and positive thinking.

3. Political Career:

In addition to his success in bodybuilding and acting, Schwarzenegger also ventured into politics. He served as the 38th governor of California from 2003 to 2011. His decision to run for office was driven by his desire to make a positive impact on society, and he applied the same principles of visualization and positive thinking to his political career. As governor, he focused on issues such as climate change, healthcare reform, and fiscal responsibility.

4. Entrepreneurship and Philanthropy:

Schwarzenegger's success extended beyond bodybuilding, acting, and politics. He became a successful entrepreneur, investing in real estate, fitness businesses, and other ventures. He also dedicated himself to philanthropy, supporting initiatives related to after-school programs, health and fitness, and environmental conservation.

Practical Insights from Arnold Schwarzenegger's Journey

Arnold Schwarzenegger's journey offers valuable lessons for anyone looking to apply the Law of Attraction in their own lives. Here are some practical insights:

1. Visualize Your Goals:

Take time each day to visualize your goals with clarity and detail. Imagine yourself achieving your dreams and experiencing the associated emotions. This practice helps align your thoughts and actions with your intentions.

2. Use Affirmations:

Create positive affirmations that reinforce your beliefs and goals. Repeat them daily to build confidence and maintain focus. For example, you might say, "I am capable of achieving my dreams," or "I attract success and abundance into my life."

3. Maintain a Positive Mindset:

Cultivate a positive mindset by focusing on opportunities for growth and learning in every experience. When faced with challenges, remind yourself that setbacks are temporary and can be overcome with perseverance and determination.

4. Surround Yourself with Positivity:

Surround yourself with positive influences, including supportive people, inspiring books, and uplifting environments. This helps reinforce your positive beliefs and keeps you motivated.

5. Take Action:

While positive thinking and visualization are important, they must be coupled with action. Take consistent steps toward your goals, and trust that your efforts will lead to success.

Arnold Schwarzenegger's story is a powerful testament to the transformative power of the Law of Attraction. By visualizing his success, using affirmations, and maintaining a positive mindset, he rose above his challenging circumstances to achieve extraordinary success in bodybuilding, acting, politics, and entrepreneurship. His journey offers inspiration and practical insights for anyone seeking to harness the power of positive thinking and achieve their dreams. As you continue exploring the Law of

Attraction, let Arnold Schwarzenegger's story guide and motivate you on your own path to success and fulfillment.

Sara Blakely

Background

Sara Blakely, the founder of Spanx, turned a simple idea into a billion-dollar business and became one of the youngest self-made female billionaires. Before achieving remarkable success, Blakely faced numerous rejections and financial struggles. Her journey from selling fax machines door-to-door to revolutionizing the women's undergarment industry showcases the power of the Law of Attraction, visualization, and positive thinking.

Early Life and Challenges

Sara Blakely was born on February 27, 1971, in Clearwater, Florida. From a young age, Blakely exhibited an entrepreneurial spirit and a determination to succeed. However, her early career was marked by a series of challenges and setbacks.

After graduating from Florida State University with a degree in communications, Blakely had aspirations of becoming a lawyer. However, she struggled with the LSAT and ultimately decided to change her career path. She took a job selling fax machines door-to-door, an experience that taught her resilience and the importance of maintaining a positive attitude despite constant rejection.

The Birth of Spanx

The idea for Spanx was born out of Blakely's personal frustration with traditional women's undergarments. She wanted to create a product that would provide a smooth, flattering look under white pants without visible panty lines. With no background in fashion or manufacturing, Blakely set out to turn her idea into reality.

1. Visualization and Positive Thinking:

Blakely consistently visualized her product becoming a success. She imagined women all over the world wearing Spanx and feeling confident and comfortable. This vision kept her motivated and focused on her goal, even when faced with numerous challenges.

2. Affirmations and Self-Belief:

Blakely used affirmations to build her confidence and reinforce her belief in her idea. She would tell herself, "I am creating a product that will change women's lives," and "I am capable of achieving great success." These affirmations helped her stay positive and determined, even when she encountered skepticism and rejection.

3. Persistence and Resilience:

Despite facing rejection from potential manufacturers and investors, Blakely remained persistent. She continued to refine her product, pitch her idea, and seek out opportunities. Her resilience and unwavering belief in her vision were crucial in overcoming the obstacles she faced.

Achieving Extraordinary Success

Sara Blakely's dedication to the Law of Attraction, visualization, and positive thinking led to her achieving extraordinary success. Here are some key milestones in her journey:

1. Initial Breakthrough:

After numerous rejections, Blakely finally found a manufacturer willing to produce her product. She invested her life savings of $5,000 to create the first prototype of Spanx. Her determination and belief in her product paid off when she secured a meeting with a buyer from Neiman Marcus. During the meeting, Blakely demonstrated the effectiveness of Spanx by modeling the product herself, impressing the buyer and securing her first major retail order.

2. Rapid Growth:

Spanx quickly gained popularity and positive word-of-mouth from satisfied customers. Oprah Winfrey featured Spanx as one of her "Favorite Things" in 2000, providing a significant boost to the brand's visibility and credibility. This exposure led to increased sales and widespread recognition.

3. Building a Billion-Dollar Business:

Blakely continued to innovate and expand the Spanx product line, introducing new styles and expanding into international markets. Her ability to maintain a clear vision, stay positive, and adapt to changing circumstances allowed her to build Spanx into a billion-dollar business.

4. Philanthropy and Empowerment:

In addition to her business success, Blakely is dedicated to philanthropy and empowering women. She founded the Sara Blakely Foundation, which supports organizations focused on education and entrepreneurship for women. Blakely's commitment to giving back and making a positive impact is an integral part of her success story.

Practical Insights from Sara Blakely's Journey

Sara Blakely's journey offers valuable lessons for anyone looking to apply the Law of Attraction in their own lives. Here are some practical insights:

1. Visualize Your Goals:

Take time each day to visualize your goals with clarity and detail. Imagine yourself achieving your dreams and experiencing the associated emotions. This practice helps align your thoughts and actions with your intentions.

2. Use Affirmations:

Create positive affirmations that reinforce your beliefs and goals. Repeat them daily to build confidence and maintain focus. For example, you might say, "I am capable of achieving my dreams," or "I attract success and abundance into my life."

3. Maintain a Positive Mindset:

Cultivate a positive mindset by focusing on opportunities for growth and learning in every experience. When faced with challenges, remind yourself that setbacks are temporary and can be overcome with perseverance and determination.

4. Stay Persistent and Resilient:

Persistence is key to achieving your goals. Stay resilient in the face of rejection and continue to refine your approach. Believe in your vision and keep moving forward, even when the path is difficult.

5. Innovate and Adapt:

Be open to innovation and adapt to changing circumstances. Continuously look for ways to improve your product or service and stay ahead of the competition.

Sara Blakely's story is a powerful testament to the transformative power of the Law of Attraction. By visualizing her success, using affirmations, and maintaining a positive mindset, she turned a simple idea into a billion-dollar business. Her journey offers inspiration and practical insights for anyone seeking to harness the power of positive thinking and achieve their dreams. As you continue exploring the Law of Attraction, let Sara Blakely's story guide and motivate you on your own path to success and fulfillment.

Will Smith

Background

Will Smith, a successful actor, producer, and musician, has often spoken about the power of positive thinking and the Law of Attraction in his career. From his early days in West Philadelphia to becoming one of Hollywood's most bankable stars, Smith's journey is a testament to the transformative power of mindset and belief. Despite facing financial difficulties and career setbacks, Smith leveraged the Law of Attraction to overcome obstacles and achieve extraordinary success.

Early Life and Challenges

Willard Carroll Smith Jr. was born on September 25, 1968, in Philadelphia, Pennsylvania. Raised in a middle-class family, Smith developed a passion for music and performance at a young age. He gained initial fame as the "Fresh Prince" in the hip-hop duo DJ Jazzy Jeff & The Fresh Prince, known for hits like "Parents Just Don't Understand" and "Summertime."

Despite early success in music, Smith faced significant financial difficulties due to poor financial management and a hefty tax debt. By the early 1990s, he was nearly bankrupt. However, Smith's charisma and talent caught the attention of television producers, leading to his breakthrough role in the popular sitcom "The Fresh Prince of Bel-Air."

The Role of the Law of Attraction

Will Smith's belief in the Law of Attraction has been a driving force throughout his career. He attributes much of his success to his ability to visualize his goals, maintain a positive mindset, and act with confidence and determination.

1. Visualization and Positive Thinking:

Smith is a strong advocate of visualization. He frequently imagined himself achieving his dreams and experiencing success. By visualizing his desired outcomes, he aligned his thoughts and actions with his goals, creating a powerful momentum toward their realization.

2. Affirmations and Self-Belief:

Smith used affirmations to reinforce his self-belief and maintain a positive attitude. He often declared his intentions and capabilities, saying things like, "I am the best" and "I create my own reality." These affirmations helped him stay focused and confident, even in challenging times.

3. Maintaining a Positive Mindset:

Smith's unwavering positive mindset has been instrumental in his journey. He believes in the power of perspective and chooses to focus on opportunities rather than obstacles. This outlook has enabled him to turn setbacks into stepping stones and continuously strive for excellence.

Achieving Extraordinary Success

Will Smith's dedication to the Law of Attraction and his unwavering belief in his dreams led to his achieving extraordinary success across multiple domains. Here are some key milestones in his journey:

1. Television Stardom:

"The Fresh Prince of Bel-Air" became a cultural phenomenon, running for six successful seasons and establishing Smith as a household name. The show's success provided a platform for Smith to transition into film.

2. Hollywood Blockbusters:

Smith's visualization and positive thinking translated into a successful film career. He starred in blockbuster films such as "Independence Day," "Men in Black," "Bad Boys," and "Ali." His ability to envision his success and maintain a positive mindset helped him become one of Hollywood's most bankable actors.

3. Music Achievements:

In addition to his acting career, Smith continued to achieve success in music. He released solo albums, including hits like "Gettin' Jiggy wit It" and "Wild Wild West." His music career earned him multiple Grammy Awards and solidified his status as a versatile entertainer.

4. Production Ventures:

Smith expanded his influence by founding Overbrook Entertainment, a production company that has produced successful films and television shows. His entrepreneurial spirit and belief in the Law of Attraction have enabled him to create and control his own projects.

5. Philanthropy and Advocacy:

Smith is also dedicated to philanthropy and advocacy. Alongside his wife, Jada Pinkett Smith, he founded the Will and Jada Smith Family Foundation, which supports education, arts, and social causes. His commitment to giving back and making a positive impact reflects his belief in creating a better reality for others.

Practical Insights from Will Smith's Journey

Will Smith's journey offers valuable lessons for anyone looking to apply the Law of Attraction in their own lives. Here are some practical insights:

1. Visualize Your Goals:

Take time each day to visualize your goals with clarity and detail. Imagine yourself achieving your dreams and experiencing the associated emotions. This practice helps align your thoughts and actions with your intentions.

2. Use Affirmations:

Create positive affirmations that reinforce your beliefs and goals. Repeat them daily to build confidence and maintain focus. For example, you might say, "I am capable of achieving my dreams," or "I attract success and abundance into my life."

3. Maintain a Positive Mindset:

Cultivate a positive mindset by focusing on opportunities for growth and learning in every experience. When faced with challenges, remind yourself that setbacks are temporary and can be overcome with perseverance and determination.

4. Surround Yourself with Positivity:

Surround yourself with positive influences, including supportive people, inspiring books, and uplifting environments. This helps reinforce your positive beliefs and keeps you motivated.

5. Take Action:

While positive thinking and visualization are important, they must be coupled with action. Take consistent steps toward your goals, and trust that your efforts will lead to success.

Will Smith's story is a powerful testament to the transformative power of the Law of Attraction. By visualizing his success, using affirmations, and maintaining a positive mindset, he rose above his challenging circumstances to become one of the most successful and influential entertainers in the world. His journey offers inspiration and practical insights for anyone seeking to harness the power of positive thinking and achieve their dreams. As you continue exploring the Law of Attraction, let Will Smith's story guide and motivate you on your own path to success and fulfillment.

CHAPTER 02

THE LAW OF CAUSE AND EFFECT

Understanding Karma

The Law of Cause and Effect, often referred to as karma, is a fundamental principle that dictates that every action has a corresponding reaction. This concept is deeply rooted in various spiritual and philosophical traditions, emphasizing the importance of conscious actions and decisions. In this chapter, we will explore the ethical and spiritual dimensions of karma, its implications for our lives, and how understanding this law can guide us toward a more mindful and purposeful existence.

The Concept of Karma

Karma is a Sanskrit word that translates to "action" or "deed." In its most basic form, it signifies the cause-and-effect relationship that governs our actions and their outcomes. The idea is that every action we take—whether good or bad—creates an energy that will eventually return to us in some form. This return may occur immediately, or it may take time, but it is inevitable.

Key Principles of Karma:

1. Moral Cause and Effect: Every action, thought, and intention creates a corresponding result. Positive actions lead to positive outcomes, while negative actions lead to negative outcomes.

2. Ethical Responsibility: Individuals are responsible for their actions and must face the consequences of their behavior, whether in this life or future lives.

3. Interconnectedness: Karma highlights the interconnectedness of all beings. Our actions impact not only ourselves but also others and the world around us.

The Ethical Dimension of Karma

Karma serves as a moral compass, guiding individuals toward ethical behavior and conscious decision-making. By understanding the law of karma, we become more aware of the impact of our actions and are encouraged to act with integrity, compassion, and mindfulness.

Ethical Implications of Karma:

1. Accountability: Karma teaches us that we are accountable for our actions. Understanding that our deeds have consequences encourages us to act responsibly and consider the ethical implications of our choices.

2. Compassion: Recognizing that our actions affect others fosters a sense of compassion and empathy. We become more mindful of how we treat people and strive to act with kindness and understanding.

3. Integrity: Karma promotes living with integrity. When we understand that our actions have long-term consequences, we are more likely to make decisions that align with our values and principles.

The Spiritual Dimension of Karma

Beyond its ethical implications, karma also has profound spiritual significance. It is a central concept in many spiritual traditions, including Hinduism, Buddhism, and Jainism, where it is seen as a force that influences the cycle of birth, death, and rebirth (samsara). Understanding karma from a spiritual perspective can lead to greater self-awareness and spiritual growth.

Spiritual Implications of Karma:

1. Self-Reflection: Karma encourages introspection and self-reflection. By examining our actions and their

outcomes, we gain insights into our behavior patterns and areas for personal growth.

2. Detachment: In spiritual practice, karma teaches the importance of detachment from the fruits of our actions. By focusing on the process rather than the outcome, we cultivate a sense of inner peace and contentment.

3. Reincarnation: In traditions that believe in reincarnation, karma is seen as a force that determines the circumstances of future lives. Positive actions in this life lead to favorable conditions in future lives, while negative actions result in challenges and suffering.

Practical Applications of Understanding Karma

Applying the principles of karma in our daily lives involves conscious decision-making and a commitment to ethical and compassionate behavior. Here are some practical ways to integrate the understanding of karma into our actions:

1. Mindful Decision-Making:

- Before taking any action, consider the potential consequences for yourself and others. Ask yourself if your actions align with your values and if they will create positive or negative outcomes.

- Practice mindfulness to stay present and aware of your thoughts, intentions, and actions.

2. Cultivating Positive Actions:

- Engage in acts of kindness, generosity, and compassion. Small positive actions can create significant ripple effects, benefiting both you and those around you.

- Practice gratitude and appreciation for the good in your life, and express this gratitude through your actions.

3. Self-Reflection and Growth:

- Regularly reflect on your actions and their outcomes. Consider what you can learn from both positive and negative experiences.

- Use introspection to identify patterns in your behavior and make conscious efforts to improve and grow.

4. Detachment and Acceptance:

- Focus on the quality of your actions rather than the outcomes. Understand that while you can control your actions, you cannot always control the results.

- Practice acceptance and let go of attachment to specific outcomes. Trust that the universe will bring the appropriate consequences based on your actions.

Real-Life Examples of Karma

Understanding karma can be enriched by examining real-life examples of how the law of cause and effect plays out. Here are a few illustrative stories:

1. The Generous Businessman:

- A successful businessman consistently donated a portion of his earnings to charitable causes. Over time, his business continued to flourish, and he gained a reputation as a kind and generous individual. His acts of generosity created positive energy that returned to him in the form of continued success and goodwill from his community.

2. The Compassionate Leader:

- A community leader who always acted with compassion and fairness found that people were willing to support and follow him during challenging times. His ethical and compassionate actions built trust and loyalty, creating a positive environment that benefited everyone involved.

3. The Dishonest Employee:

- An employee who consistently lied and manipulated colleagues for personal gain eventually faced serious consequences. His actions led to mistrust and conflict in the workplace, and he was ultimately fired. The negative energy he created through his dishonesty returned to him, demonstrating the principle of karma in action.

The Law of Cause and Effect, or karma, is a powerful principle that underscores the importance of our actions and decisions. By understanding karma, we become more aware of the ethical and spiritual dimensions of our behavior, encouraging us to act with integrity, compassion, and mindfulness. Integrating the principles of karma into our daily lives can lead to personal growth, positive relationships, and a more harmonious existence. As we continue exploring the Law of Cause and Effect, let this understanding of karma guide us toward a more conscious and purposeful life.

Ethical Living

Moral Decision-Making: Strategies for Making Choices that Align with One's Values

Ethical living involves making choices that reflect our core values and principles. Moral decision-making is a crucial aspect of this, as it requires us to consider the ethical implications of our actions and strive to do what is right. By aligning our decisions with our values, we can create positive outcomes for ourselves and others. This chapter explores strategies for moral decision-making, offering practical guidance on how to navigate complex ethical dilemmas and live a life of integrity.

Understanding Moral Decision-Making

Moral decision-making is the process of evaluating and choosing actions that are consistent with ethical principles and personal values. It involves:

1.   Recognizing Ethical Dilemmas: Identifying situations where a choice must be made between competing values or principles.

2. Evaluating Options: Considering the potential consequences and ethical implications of different actions.

3. Making Informed Choices: Selecting actions that align with one's values and ethical standards.

4. Taking Responsibility: Being accountable for the outcomes of one's decisions and actions.

Key Principles of Moral Decision-Making

1. Integrity: Acting consistently with your values and ethical principles, even when it is difficult or inconvenient.

2. Honesty: Being truthful and transparent in your actions and communications.

3. Respect: Treating others with dignity and consideration, recognizing their inherent worth.

4. Fairness: Making decisions that are just and equitable, avoiding favoritism or discrimination.

5. Compassion: Considering the impact of your actions on others and striving to alleviate suffering.

Strategies for Moral Decision-Making

To make moral decisions that align with your values, consider the following strategies:

1. Clarify Your Values:

- Take time to reflect on your core values and principles. What matters most to you? What ethical standards do you strive to uphold?

- Write down your values and keep them in mind when making decisions. This can serve as a guide to ensure your actions are aligned with your principles.

2. Gather Information:

- Before making a decision, gather relevant information to understand the context and potential consequences. This includes considering the perspectives and needs of those affected by your decision.

- Seek input from trusted advisors, mentors, or colleagues to gain different viewpoints and insights.

3. Evaluate the Consequences:

- Consider the short-term and long-term consequences of each option. How will your decision impact yourself and others? What are the potential benefits and harms?

- Use a pros and cons list to weigh the advantages and disadvantages of each option.

4. Consider Ethical Principles:

- Apply ethical principles such as honesty, fairness, and compassion to your decision-making process. How do these principles influence your choice?

- Use ethical frameworks, such as utilitarianism (maximizing overall happiness) or deontology (adhering to moral duties), to guide your evaluation of options.

5. Reflect on Past Experiences:

- Reflect on previous decisions and their outcomes. What lessons did you learn? How can these insights inform your current decision?

- Consider how your past actions align with your values and what changes you might need to make to improve your moral decision-making.

6. Imagine the Impact:

- Visualize the potential impact of your decision on all stakeholders. How would you feel if you were in their position? How would you want to be treated?

- Use empathy to understand the emotional and practical consequences of your actions on others.

7. Seek Alignment with Your Purpose:

- Ensure that your decisions align with your broader life purpose and goals. Are your choices contributing to your overall mission and vision?

- Consider how your actions reflect your commitment to your values and ethical standards.

8. Consult Ethical Guidelines:

- Refer to ethical guidelines or codes of conduct relevant to your profession or organization. These can provide valuable insights and standards for ethical behavior.

- Ensure your decisions comply with legal and regulatory requirements.

9. Use a Decision-Making Model:

- Employ structured decision-making models to guide your process. One such model is the PLUS Decision-Making Model, which includes the following steps:

- Policies: Does the decision align with organizational policies?

- Legal: Is the decision compliant with laws and regulations?

- Universal: Does the decision uphold universal ethical principles?

- Self: Does the decision align with your personal values and standards?

10. Take Responsibility:

- Accept responsibility for your decisions and their outcomes. Be prepared to explain and justify your choices based on your values and ethical principles.

- Learn from your experiences and be willing to make amends if your decisions cause harm.

Practical Examples of Moral Decision-Making

Understanding moral decision-making can be enriched by examining real-life examples of how ethical principles are applied in various contexts:

1. Business Leadership:

- A CEO faced with the decision to lay off employees to cut costs might consider alternatives such as reducing executive salaries or implementing temporary furloughs. By prioritizing fairness and compassion, the CEO seeks to minimize harm to employees while addressing financial challenges.

2. Healthcare:

- A doctor must decide whether to provide a costly treatment to a patient with limited insurance coverage. The doctor considers the patient's well-being, the ethical principle of beneficence (acting in the patient's best interest), and the potential financial burden. The decision balances medical ethics with practical considerations.

3. Environmental Responsibility:

- A company deciding whether to invest in sustainable practices evaluates the long-term environmental impact, the ethical duty to protect the planet, and the potential benefits for future generations. The decision reflects a commitment to environmental stewardship and corporate social responsibility.

4. Personal Relationships:

- An individual deciding whether to be honest with a friend about a difficult truth considers the principles of honesty and respect. The decision involves weighing the potential harm of the truth against the value of transparency and trust in the relationship.

Moral decision-making is an essential aspect of ethical living, requiring us to evaluate our choices and actions in light of our values and ethical principles. By clarifying our values, gathering information, considering consequences, and applying ethical frameworks, we can make informed decisions that align with our commitment to integrity, honesty, respect, fairness, and compassion. As we continue exploring the Law of Cause and Effect, let these strategies for moral decision-making guide us toward a more ethical and purposeful life, creating positive outcomes for ourselves and others.

Consequences and Responsibility: Understanding the Long-Term Impacts of Actions

The Law of Cause and Effect, or karma, emphasizes that every action we take has consequences that can affect our lives and the lives of others. Understanding the long-term impacts of our actions is crucial for making ethical decisions and taking responsibility for our behaviors. This chapter explores the concept of consequences and responsibility, highlighting the importance of mindful actions and the ways in which they shape our future.

The Nature of Consequences

Consequences are the results or outcomes that follow from our actions, decisions, and behaviors. They can be immediate or delayed, positive or negative, and can affect various aspects of our lives, including our relationships, careers, health, and overall well-being. Recognizing the potential consequences of our actions helps us make more informed and ethical choices.

Types of Consequences:

1. Immediate Consequences: These are the direct and immediate results of our actions. For example, studying hard for an exam results in good grades, while neglecting health can lead to immediate illness.

2. Long-Term Consequences: These are the delayed outcomes that arise from our actions over time. For example, saving money consistently leads to financial security, while engaging in unhealthy habits can result in chronic health issues.

3. Positive Consequences: These are beneficial outcomes that result from ethical and responsible actions.

They contribute to our well-being and the well-being of others.

4. Negative Consequences: These are harmful outcomes that result from unethical or irresponsible actions. They can cause suffering, conflict, and damage to ourselves and others.

The Importance of Responsibility

Responsibility is the acknowledgment and acceptance of the consequences of our actions. It involves being accountable for our behavior and understanding that our choices have an impact on our lives and the lives of others. Taking responsibility fosters personal growth, ethical living, and positive relationships.

Key Aspects of Responsibility:

1. Self-Awareness: Recognizing the impact of our actions and understanding our role in creating outcomes.

2. Accountability: Accepting ownership of our decisions and their consequences, whether positive or negative.

3. Ethical Behavior: Making choices that align with our values and principles, and considering the broader impact of our actions.

4. Learning and Growth: Reflecting on our experiences, learning from our mistakes, and striving to improve our behavior.

Strategies for Understanding and Managing Consequences

To effectively manage the consequences of our actions and take responsibility, consider the following strategies:

1. Reflect on Past Actions:

- Reflect on previous decisions and their outcomes. Consider how your actions have influenced your life and the lives of others.

- Identify patterns in your behavior and their consequences, and use this insight to guide future decisions.

2. Consider the Ripple Effect:

- Understand that your actions can have a ripple effect, influencing not only immediate outcomes but also the broader environment and community.

- Think about how your decisions might impact others, including family, friends, colleagues, and society as a whole.

3. Evaluate Long-Term Impact:

- When making decisions, consider both the short-term and long-term consequences. Ask yourself how your choices will affect your future and the future of those around you.

- Use tools such as pros and cons lists to weigh the potential benefits and risks of different actions.

4. Practice Mindfulness:

- Cultivate mindfulness to stay present and aware of your thoughts, intentions, and actions. Mindfulness helps you make conscious choices rather than reacting impulsively.

- Regularly check in with yourself to ensure your actions align with your values and ethical principles.

5. Seek Guidance and Feedback:

- Consult with trusted advisors, mentors, or peers when facing difficult decisions. Seeking diverse perspectives can help you understand the potential consequences more fully.

- Be open to feedback and constructive criticism, and use it to improve your decision-making process.

6. Accept Responsibility:

- Take ownership of your actions and their outcomes. If your decisions lead to negative consequences, acknowledge your role and take steps to make amends.

- Celebrate positive outcomes and recognize the impact of your responsible and ethical behavior.

7. Learn from Experience:

- Reflect on both positive and negative experiences to gain insights and improve your behavior. Consider what you can learn from each situation and how you can apply these lessons in the future.

- Use mistakes as opportunities for growth and development, rather than as sources of guilt or shame.

Real-Life Examples of Consequences and Responsibility

Understanding the importance of consequences and responsibility can be enriched by examining real-life examples of how individuals have managed their actions and their outcomes:

1. Corporate Accountability:

- A company faced with environmental violations decides to take responsibility by implementing sustainable practices and addressing the harm caused. This decision not only improves the company's reputation but also contributes to the well-being of the community and the environment.

2. Personal Health:

- An individual who neglected their health for years experiences a serious health scare. Recognizing the long-term consequences of their lifestyle, they take responsibility by adopting healthier habits, seeking medical advice, and committing to regular exercise and a balanced diet.

3. Leadership and Integrity:

   - A political leader who made a controversial decision that led to public discontent publicly acknowledges the mistake, explains the rationale behind the decision, and takes steps to address the concerns of the affected population. This act of responsibility helps restore trust and credibility.

4. Community Involvement:

   - A community member who previously ignored local issues decides to get involved and contribute to positive change. By volunteering and advocating for improvements, they help create a better environment for everyone, demonstrating the long-term impact of responsible actions.

The Law of Cause and Effect underscores the importance of understanding the consequences of our actions and taking responsibility for them. By recognizing the long-term impacts of our decisions, we can make more informed and ethical choices that align with our values and contribute to the well-being of ourselves and others. Embracing responsibility fosters personal growth, ethical living, and positive relationships, guiding us toward a more mindful and purposeful life. As we continue exploring the Law of Cause and Effect, let these strategies for understanding and managing consequences help us create a positive and lasting impact on our lives and the world around us.

Personal Accountability: Developing a Sense of Responsibility for One's Actions

Personal accountability is the foundation of ethical living and a key component of the Law of Cause and Effect. It involves taking responsibility for our actions, decisions, and their consequences. By developing a strong sense of personal accountability, we can foster integrity, build trust, and create a positive impact in our lives and the lives of others. This chapter delves into the concept of personal accountability, its importance, and strategies for cultivating it in our daily lives.

Understanding Personal Accountability

Personal accountability means recognizing and accepting responsibility for our actions and their outcomes. It requires honesty, self-awareness, and a commitment to ethical behavior. When we hold ourselves accountable, we acknowledge our role in shaping our lives and take proactive steps to align our actions with our values.

Key Aspects of Personal Accountability:

1. Self-Awareness: Understanding our thoughts, emotions, and behaviors and how they influence our actions.

2. Honesty: Being truthful with ourselves and others about our actions and their consequences.

3. Responsibility: Accepting ownership of our decisions and their outcomes, both positive and negative.

4. Proactivity: Taking initiative to address issues, make amends, and improve our behavior.

5. Learning and Growth: Using experiences, including mistakes, as opportunities for personal development and growth.

The Importance of Personal Accountability

Personal accountability is crucial for several reasons:

1. Integrity and Trust: Holding ourselves accountable builds integrity and trust. People are more likely to respect and trust us when we take responsibility for our actions.

2. Ethical Behavior: Accountability promotes ethical behavior by encouraging us to consider the consequences of our actions and make decisions that align with our values.

3. Personal Growth: Accepting responsibility for our actions helps us learn from our experiences and fosters personal growth and development.

4. Positive Relationships: Accountability strengthens relationships by fostering open communication, mutual respect, and trust.

Strategies for Developing Personal Accountability

To cultivate a strong sense of personal accountability, consider the following strategies:

1. Self-Reflection:

- Regularly reflect on your actions, decisions, and their outcomes. Consider how your behavior aligns with your values and what you can learn from your experiences.

- Use journaling or meditation to enhance self-awareness and gain insights into your actions and motivations.

2. Set Clear Expectations:

- Clearly define your goals, responsibilities, and standards for behavior. Understand what is expected of you in different areas of your life, including work, relationships, and personal development.

- Communicate your expectations to others and ensure that you understand their expectations of you.

3. Own Your Decisions:

- Take ownership of your decisions and their outcomes. Avoid blaming others or making excuses for your actions.

- When things go wrong, acknowledge your role in the situation and take responsibility for addressing any issues.

4. Follow Through on Commitments:

- Honor your commitments and promises. If you agree to do something, ensure that you follow through and complete it to the best of your ability.

- If you are unable to fulfill a commitment, communicate openly and honestly, and take steps to make amends.

5. Seek Feedback:

- Actively seek feedback from others to gain different perspectives on your behavior and performance. Use this feedback to identify areas for improvement and make necessary changes.

- Be open to constructive criticism and view it as an opportunity for growth.

6. Develop a Growth Mindset:

- Embrace a growth mindset by viewing challenges and setbacks as opportunities for learning and development. Understand that mistakes are a natural part of the learning process.

- Focus on continuous improvement and strive to enhance your skills, knowledge, and behavior.

7. Practice Honesty and Transparency:

- Be honest and transparent with yourself and others about your actions, decisions, and their outcomes. Avoid hiding mistakes or shifting blame.

- Openly acknowledge your successes and failures, and take responsibility for your role in both.

8. Establish Accountability Partners:

- Find accountability partners, such as friends, colleagues, or mentors, who can support you in your journey toward greater accountability. Share your goals and progress with them, and seek their guidance and feedback.

- Hold each other accountable by regularly checking in on progress and providing mutual support.

9. Create an Accountability Plan:

- Develop a personal accountability plan that outlines your goals, responsibilities, and strategies for maintaining accountability. Include specific actions you will take to stay accountable and address any challenges that arise.

- Review and update your plan regularly to ensure that it remains relevant and effective.

Real-Life Examples of Personal Accountability

Understanding the importance of personal accountability can be enriched by examining real-life examples of individuals who have demonstrated this quality:

1. Professional Accountability:

- A project manager who missed a critical deadline takes responsibility by acknowledging the oversight, analyzing the reasons for the delay, and implementing measures to prevent future occurrences. This proactive approach builds trust with the team and clients.

2. Personal Accountability in Relationships:

- A partner who realizes they have been neglecting their relationship takes responsibility by acknowledging their behavior, apologizing, and making a concerted effort to spend more quality time with their partner. This accountability strengthens the relationship and fosters mutual respect.

3. Community Involvement:

- A community leader who recognizes a mistake in organizing an event takes responsibility by addressing the issue, seeking feedback from the community, and making necessary improvements for future events. This accountability enhances the leader's credibility and trust within the community.

4. Health and Wellness:

- An individual who realizes they have been neglecting their health takes responsibility by acknowledging their behavior, seeking medical advice, and committing to a healthier lifestyle. This accountability leads to improved well-being and sets a positive example for others.

Personal accountability is a fundamental aspect of ethical living and a key component of the Law of Cause and Effect. By developing a sense of responsibility for our actions, we can build integrity, trust, and positive relationships. Strategies such as self-reflection, setting clear expectations, owning our decisions, and seeking feedback can help us cultivate personal accountability and align our actions with our values. As we continue exploring the Law of Cause and Effect, let these strategies guide us toward a more responsible and purposeful life, creating positive outcomes for ourselves and the world around us.

Real-Life Examples: Accounts of How Individuals' Actions Have Led to Significant Consequences

Understanding the Law of Cause and Effect through real-life examples helps to illustrate the profound impact our actions can have on our lives and the lives of others. By examining both positive and negative outcomes, we can better appreciate the importance of mindful behavior and personal accountability. This chapter presents a series of real-life stories that highlight the consequences of actions and the critical role of ethical decision-making.

Positive Consequences

1. Malala Yousafzai: Advocacy for Education

Background:

Malala Yousafzai, a Pakistani activist for female education, became an international symbol of the fight for girls' rights. Growing up in a region where the Taliban often banned girls from attending school, Malala's advocacy for education faced extreme opposition.

Actions:

Malala spoke out publicly about the importance of education for girls, writing blogs for the BBC and giving interviews. Despite threats from the Taliban, she continued her advocacy, believing in the right to education for all.

Consequences:

In 2012, Malala survived an assassination attempt by the Taliban, which garnered global attention. Her bravery and unwavering commitment to education inspired millions worldwide. She received numerous accolades, including the Nobel Peace Prize in 2014. Malala's actions have led to increased awareness and support for girls' education globally, illustrating the positive impact of courageous and principled behavior.

2. Elon Musk: Innovation and Sustainability

Background:

Elon Musk, an entrepreneur and inventor, is known for his role in revolutionizing multiple industries, including electric vehicles and space exploration. His vision for a sustainable future has driven many of his ventures.

Actions:

Musk founded Tesla, Inc., with the goal of accelerating the world's transition to sustainable energy. He also founded SpaceX, aiming to reduce space transportation costs and enable the colonization of Mars. Through his companies, Musk has pushed the boundaries of technology and innovation.

Consequences:

Tesla has become a leader in the electric vehicle market, significantly reducing carbon emissions and promoting renewable energy. SpaceX has achieved groundbreaking advancements in space travel, including the first privately funded spacecraft to reach orbit and return. Musk's actions have had a transformative impact on the automotive and aerospace industries, promoting sustainability and technological progress.

Negative Consequences

1. Enron Scandal: Corporate Fraud and Its Fallout

Background:

Enron Corporation was an American energy company that became infamous for its involvement in one of the largest corporate fraud scandals in history. Executives at Enron engaged in unethical practices to hide the company's financial losses and inflate its stock price.

Actions:

Enron executives used complex accounting loopholes and special purpose entities to conceal debt and artificially boost earnings. They misled investors, employees, and the public about the company's financial health.

Consequences:

When the fraud was exposed in 2001, Enron filed for bankruptcy, leading to significant financial losses for shareholders and employees. Thousands of employees lost their jobs and retirement savings. The scandal also led to increased regulatory scrutiny and the creation of the Sarbanes-Oxley Act to improve corporate governance and accountability. The Enron case serves as a stark reminder of the destructive impact of unethical behavior.

2. Volkswagen Emissions Scandal: Deception and Environmental Harm

Background:

Volkswagen (VW), one of the world's largest automobile manufacturers, was found to have installed software in its diesel vehicles to cheat emissions tests. This deception allowed the vehicles to meet regulatory standards while emitting pollutants well above legal limits during normal operation.

Actions:

VW engineers developed and installed "defeat devices" in diesel engines, which could detect when the vehicle was undergoing emissions testing and temporarily reduce emissions to comply with regulations. During regular driving conditions, the vehicles emitted nitrogen oxides at levels up to 40 times the legal limit.

Consequences:

The scandal, revealed in 2015, led to significant legal and financial repercussions for VW, including billions of dollars in fines and settlements. The company's reputation was severely damaged, and the scandal had wide-ranging environmental and public health impacts. The VW case highlights the long-term negative consequences of unethical corporate behavior and the importance of transparency and integrity.

Mixed Consequences

1. Edward Snowden: Whistleblowing and Public Debate

Background:

Edward Snowden, a former contractor for the National Security Agency (NSA), became a controversial figure when he leaked classified information revealing the extent of global surveillance programs conducted by the NSA and other intelligence agencies.

Actions:

In 2013, Snowden disclosed documents to journalists detailing mass surveillance practices, including the collection of phone and internet data from millions of individuals without their knowledge or consent. He believed the public had a right to know about these programs and fled the United States to avoid prosecution.

Consequences:

Snowden's actions sparked a global debate about privacy, government surveillance, and civil liberties. While some view him as a hero for exposing government overreach, others see him as a traitor who compromised national security. His disclosures led to increased transparency and reforms in surveillance practices but also resulted in his exile and legal battles. The Snowden case illustrates the complex interplay of ethics, legality, and the public interest.

2. Mark Zuckerberg: Innovation and Ethical Challenges

Background:

Mark Zuckerberg, co-founder and CEO of Facebook, has played a pivotal role in transforming social media and digital communication. Facebook's rapid growth has connected billions of people worldwide and revolutionized how information is shared.

Actions:

Under Zuckerberg's leadership, Facebook has introduced numerous innovations and expanded its reach. However, the company has also faced criticism for its handling of user data, privacy concerns, and the spread of misinformation and harmful content on its platform.

Consequences:

While Facebook has had a significant positive impact on global communication and connectivity, it has also been implicated in ethical and regulatory challenges. Data breaches, such as the Cambridge Analytica scandal, and the platform's role in political manipulation have led to public backlash and calls for greater accountability. Zuckerberg's leadership highlights the dual-edged nature of technological innovation and the need for ethical considerations in business practices.

These real-life examples underscore the importance of mindful behavior and ethical decision-making. Whether the consequences are positive or negative, our actions have far-reaching impacts on our lives and the lives of others. By understanding the Law of Cause and Effect and taking responsibility for our behavior, we can strive to make choices that align with our values and contribute to a more just and compassionate world. As we continue exploring the Law of

Cause and Effect, let these stories serve as a reminder of the power of our actions and the critical role of personal accountability in shaping our future.

CHAPTER 03

THE LAW OF GROWTH

Embracing Change

Change is an inevitable and fundamental aspect of life. It drives growth, fosters learning, and enables us to adapt to new circumstances. Embracing change is essential for personal development and achieving our full potential. This chapter explores the Law of Growth, focusing on the importance of accepting and adapting to change, and provides strategies for continuously striving for self-improvement.

Understanding the Law of Growth

The Law of Growth emphasizes that personal and professional development is a lifelong process. Growth involves expanding our knowledge, skills, and understanding, as well as improving our attitudes, behaviors, and habits. Embracing change is a crucial component of this process, as it allows us to move beyond our comfort zones and reach new heights.

Key Principles of the Law of Growth:

1. Continuous Learning: Actively seeking new knowledge and experiences to enhance personal and professional development.

2. Adaptability: Being flexible and open to change, allowing us to navigate new situations and challenges effectively.

3. Self-Improvement: Consistently working to better ourselves, whether through developing new skills, improving existing ones, or cultivating positive behaviors and attitudes.

The Importance of Embracing Change

1. Opportunities for Growth: Change often brings new opportunities for learning and development. By embracing change, we can seize these opportunities and expand our horizons.

2. Resilience: Accepting and adapting to change builds resilience, enabling us to cope with adversity and bounce back from setbacks.

3. Innovation and Creativity: Change encourages us to think creatively and develop innovative solutions to

problems. This can lead to personal and professional breakthroughs.

4. Enhanced Relationships: Being open to change can improve our relationships by fostering empathy, understanding, and collaboration.

Strategies for Embracing Change

To effectively embrace change and foster growth, consider the following strategies:

1. Cultivate a Growth Mindset:

- Adopt a growth mindset by viewing challenges and setbacks as opportunities for learning and development. Understand that abilities and intelligence can be developed through effort and perseverance.

- Replace self-limiting beliefs with positive affirmations that reinforce your capacity for growth and change.

2. Set Clear Goals:

- Define clear, achievable goals that align with your values and aspirations. Break these goals into smaller, manageable steps to make the process of change less overwhelming.

- Regularly review and adjust your goals to reflect new insights and changing circumstances.

3. Seek Continuous Learning:

- Commit to lifelong learning by seeking new knowledge, skills, and experiences. This can include formal education, workshops, online courses, reading, and engaging with mentors.

- Stay curious and open-minded, and actively seek opportunities to expand your understanding and expertise.

4. Develop Adaptability:

- Practice flexibility by being open to new ideas, perspectives, and approaches. Embrace uncertainty and view it as an opportunity for growth rather than a threat.

- Cultivate resilience by developing coping strategies and maintaining a positive attitude in the face of change.

5. Embrace Failure as a Learning Opportunity:

- Recognize that failure is a natural part of the growth process. Instead of fearing failure, view it as a valuable learning experience that can provide insights and drive improvement.

- Analyze your failures to understand what went wrong, and use this knowledge to make better decisions in the future.

6. Stay Connected and Seek Support:

- Surround yourself with a supportive network of friends, family, mentors, and colleagues who encourage your growth and provide guidance during times of change.

- Share your experiences and challenges with others, and seek feedback to gain different perspectives and insights.

7. Practice Mindfulness and Reflection:

- Incorporate mindfulness practices, such as meditation and journaling, into your daily routine to enhance self-awareness and stay present in the moment.

- Regularly reflect on your experiences, goals, and progress to identify areas for improvement and celebrate your achievements.

Real-Life Examples of Embracing Change

1. Oprah Winfrey: Media Mogul and Philanthropist

- Oprah Winfrey's journey from a challenging childhood to becoming a media mogul and philanthropist exemplifies the power of embracing change. Despite facing numerous obstacles, she continuously sought new opportunities for growth and self-improvement. Oprah's ability to adapt to changing circumstances and leverage new opportunities has made her one of the most influential figures in media and philanthropy.

2. Steve Jobs: Innovator and Entrepreneur

- Steve Jobs, co-founder of Apple Inc., demonstrated the importance of embracing change and innovation. Throughout his career, Jobs faced significant setbacks, including being ousted from Apple. However, he used these experiences as opportunities for growth, eventually returning to Apple and leading the company to unprecedented success with innovative products like the iPhone and iPad.

3. Malala Yousafzai: Education Activist

- Malala Yousafzai's advocacy for girls' education in the face of adversity highlights the importance of resilience and embracing change. After surviving an assassination attempt by the Taliban, Malala continued her activism, using her experiences to drive global awareness and change. Her commitment to education and adaptability in the face of challenges have made her a powerful voice for social change.

Practical Exercises for Embracing Change

1. Change Your Routine:

- Experiment with changing your daily routine to introduce new experiences and perspectives. This can help you become more comfortable with change and develop adaptability.

- Try new activities, explore different environments, and engage with diverse groups of people to broaden your horizons.

2. Set Stretch Goals:

- Challenge yourself by setting stretch goals that push you beyond your comfort zone. These goals should be ambitious yet achievable, motivating you to strive for growth and improvement.

- Track your progress and celebrate small victories along the way to stay motivated and build confidence.

3. Engage in Reflective Practices:

- Incorporate reflective practices, such as journaling, into your daily routine to enhance self-awareness and track your growth. Reflect on your experiences, emotions, and lessons learned to gain insights and identify areas for improvement.

- Use reflection to set new goals and adjust your approach based on your experiences and evolving circumstances.

4. Develop a Personal Growth Plan:

- Create a personal growth plan that outlines your goals, strategies, and timeline for achieving them. Include specific actions you will take to embrace change and foster growth.

- Regularly review and update your plan to ensure it remains relevant and aligned with your evolving aspirations.

Embracing change is essential for personal and professional growth. By adopting a growth mindset, setting clear goals, seeking continuous learning, and developing adaptability, we can navigate change effectively and use it as a catalyst for self-improvement. Real-life examples of individuals who have embraced change highlight the transformative power of this approach. As we continue exploring the Law of Growth, let these strategies and practices guide us toward a more dynamic, resilient, and fulfilling life, where change is seen not as a threat but as an opportunity for continual growth and development.

Personal Development

Continuous Learning: Cultivating a Habit of Lifelong Learning

Lifelong learning is a cornerstone of personal development and an essential component of the Law of Growth. By continuously seeking new knowledge, skills, and experiences, we can enhance our personal and professional lives, adapt to changing circumstances, and achieve our fullest potential. This chapter explores the importance of continuous learning, its benefits, and practical strategies for cultivating a habit of lifelong learning.

The Importance of Continuous Learning

Continuous learning involves actively and consistently seeking new information and experiences to expand our understanding and abilities. It is a dynamic process that fosters personal growth and development, enabling us to stay relevant and competitive in an ever-changing world.

Key Reasons to Embrace Continuous Learning:

1. Adaptability: In a rapidly evolving world, continuous learning helps us stay adaptable and responsive to new challenges and opportunities.

2. Personal Growth: Lifelong learning promotes personal growth by enhancing our knowledge, skills, and self-awareness.

3. Professional Development: Ongoing education and skill development are crucial for career advancement and staying competitive in the job market.

4. Cognitive Health: Engaging in continuous learning activities stimulates the brain, improving cognitive function and reducing the risk of cognitive decline.

5. Fulfillment: Learning new things can bring a sense of accomplishment and fulfillment, enriching our lives and broadening our horizons.

Benefits of Continuous Learning

1. Enhanced Problem-Solving Skills:

- Continuous learning fosters critical thinking and problem-solving abilities. By exposing ourselves to diverse perspectives and knowledge, we can approach challenges more creatively and effectively.

2. Increased Confidence:

- Gaining new knowledge and skills boosts our confidence and self-esteem. This confidence translates into greater competence and effectiveness in various aspects of life.

3. Better Decision-Making:

- With a broader knowledge base, we can make more informed decisions. Continuous learning provides the tools and insights needed to evaluate options and choose the best course of action.

4. Improved Relationships:

- Lifelong learning enhances our communication and interpersonal skills, leading to better relationships with family, friends, colleagues, and peers.

5. Career Advancement:

- Staying updated with industry trends and acquiring new skills can lead to career growth and advancement opportunities. Continuous learning makes us more valuable and versatile employees.

Strategies for Cultivating a Habit of Lifelong Learning

To develop a habit of continuous learning, consider the following strategies:

1. Set Learning Goals:

- Define clear and achievable learning goals that align with your personal and professional aspirations. Break these goals into smaller, manageable steps to maintain motivation and track progress.

- Regularly review and adjust your goals to reflect your evolving interests and needs.

2. Create a Learning Plan:

- Develop a structured learning plan that outlines the topics, resources, and activities you will engage in to achieve your learning goals. Include a timeline to stay organized and focused.

- Allocate specific time slots in your daily or weekly schedule for learning activities to ensure consistency.

3. Leverage Online Resources:

- Utilize online platforms, such as Coursera, Udemy, Khan Academy, and LinkedIn Learning, to access a wide range of courses and tutorials on various subjects.

- Explore free resources, such as podcasts, webinars, and YouTube channels, to supplement your learning.

4. Read Regularly:

- Make reading a regular part of your routine. Choose books, articles, and journals that interest you and expand your knowledge.

- Join a book club or reading group to discuss and share insights with others.

5. Engage in Professional Development:

- Attend workshops, conferences, and seminars to stay updated with industry trends and network with professionals in your field.

- Pursue certifications and advanced degrees to enhance your qualifications and expertise.

6. Practice Active Learning:

- Engage in hands-on activities, such as projects, experiments, and simulations, to reinforce your learning and apply new knowledge in practical contexts.

- Participate in discussions, debates, and group activities to deepen your understanding and gain diverse perspectives.

7. Seek Feedback and Mentorship:

- Seek feedback from peers, mentors, and experts to gain insights into your strengths and areas for improvement. Use this feedback to refine your learning approach and set new goals.

- Establish relationships with mentors who can guide and support your learning journey.

8. Stay Curious and Open-Minded:

- Cultivate a curious mindset by asking questions, exploring new interests, and challenging your assumptions. Stay open to new ideas and perspectives.

- Embrace a growth mindset by viewing challenges and setbacks as opportunities for learning and development.

9. Reflect on Your Learning:

- Regularly reflect on your learning experiences to assess your progress and identify areas for improvement. Use journaling or self-assessment tools to document your insights and achievements.

- Celebrate your successes and acknowledge the effort you have invested in your growth.

Real-Life Examples of Continuous Learning

1. Warren Buffett: The Lifelong Learner

- Warren Buffett, one of the most successful investors in the world, attributes much of his success to his commitment to continuous learning. He spends a significant portion of his day reading books, newspapers, and reports to stay informed and make informed investment decisions. Buffett's dedication to learning has enabled him to adapt to changing market conditions and maintain a competitive edge.

2. Marie Curie: Pioneering Scientist

- Marie Curie, a renowned physicist and chemist, exemplified the spirit of lifelong learning. Despite facing numerous challenges as a woman in science, Curie continued to pursue her education and research, ultimately discovering radium and polonium. Her relentless pursuit of knowledge earned her two Nobel Prizes and made significant contributions to science and medicine.

3. Bill Gates: The Voracious Reader

- Bill Gates, co-founder of Microsoft, is a passionate advocate for continuous learning. He reads extensively on a wide range of topics, from technology and science to history and public health. Gates shares his reading list and insights on his blog, encouraging others to embrace lifelong learning. His commitment to learning has fueled his philanthropic efforts and innovative solutions to global challenges.

Practical Exercises for Continuous Learning

1. Daily Learning Routine:

- Set aside at least 30 minutes each day for learning activities, such as reading, taking an online course, or watching educational videos. Consistency is key to developing a habit of lifelong learning.

2. Learning Journal:

- Keep a learning journal to document your progress, insights, and reflections. Record the topics you explore, the resources you use, and the key takeaways from your learning experiences.

3. Skill Development Projects:

- Undertake projects that challenge you to apply new skills and knowledge. For example, if you are learning a new language, create a short story or presentation in that language. If you are learning coding, build a simple application or website.

4. Discussion Groups:

- Join or form discussion groups with like-minded individuals who share your interests. Engage in regular discussions to exchange ideas, ask questions, and gain diverse perspectives on various topics.

5. Lifelong Learning Plan:

- Create a comprehensive lifelong learning plan that outlines your short-term and long-term learning goals, the resources you will use, and the strategies you will employ. Review and update your plan regularly to stay on track and adjust to new interests.

Continuous learning is a vital component of personal development and the Law of Growth. By cultivating a habit of lifelong learning, we can enhance our knowledge, skills, and adaptability, leading to greater personal and professional fulfillment. Embracing strategies such as setting learning goals, leveraging online resources, practicing active learning, and seeking feedback can help us stay committed to our learning journey. Real-life examples of lifelong learners, like Warren Buffett, Marie Curie, and Bill Gates, inspire us to prioritize continuous learning and strive for continuous improvement. As we continue exploring the Law of Growth, let these strategies and practices guide us toward a more informed, capable, and enriched life.

Adaptability: Techniques for Remaining Flexible and Open to Change

Adaptability is the ability to adjust to new conditions, embrace change, and remain flexible in the face of uncertainty. In a rapidly changing world, adaptability is crucial for personal growth, professional success, and overall well-being. This chapter explores the importance of adaptability, its benefits, and practical techniques for cultivating flexibility and openness to change.

Understanding Adaptability

Adaptability involves a mindset and set of skills that enable individuals to respond effectively to new challenges and opportunities. It requires openness to new experiences, resilience in the face of adversity, and a willingness to learn and grow.

Key Components of Adaptability:

1. Openness to Change: Being receptive to new ideas, experiences, and perspectives.

2. Resilience: The ability to recover from setbacks and maintain a positive outlook.

3. Flexibility: The capacity to adjust behaviors, strategies, and attitudes to meet new demands.

4. Continuous Learning: An ongoing commitment to acquiring new knowledge and skills.

The Importance of Adaptability

Adaptability is essential for several reasons:

1. Navigating Uncertainty: In an unpredictable world, adaptability allows us to manage uncertainty and make the most of new opportunities.

2. Personal Growth: Embracing change fosters personal development and helps us reach our full potential.

3. Professional Success: Adaptability is a key competency in the workplace, enabling us to stay relevant and competitive.

4. Enhanced Relationships: Being flexible and open-minded improves our interactions with others and fosters stronger relationships.

5. Well-Being: Adaptability contributes to mental and emotional well-being by helping us cope with stress and maintain a positive outlook.

Techniques for Cultivating Adaptability

To develop adaptability, consider the following techniques:

1. Cultivate a Growth Mindset:

- Embrace the belief that abilities and intelligence can be developed through effort and learning. View challenges and setbacks as opportunities for growth.

- Replace self-limiting beliefs with positive affirmations that reinforce your capacity for change and improvement.

2. Stay Curious and Open-Minded:

- Foster curiosity by asking questions, exploring new interests, and seeking out diverse perspectives. Stay open to new ideas and experiences.

- Challenge your assumptions and be willing to reconsider your viewpoints in light of new information.

3. Practice Flexibility:

- Develop the habit of adjusting your plans and strategies in response to changing circumstances. Be willing to try new approaches and adapt your behavior as needed.

- Embrace uncertainty and view it as an opportunity for creativity and innovation.

4. Build Resilience:

- Strengthen your resilience by developing coping strategies for dealing with stress and adversity. Maintain a positive attitude and focus on solutions rather than problems.

- Practice self-care and seek support from friends, family, and mentors during challenging times.

5. Engage in Continuous Learning:

- Commit to lifelong learning by seeking new knowledge and skills. Stay informed about industry trends and developments, and pursue opportunities for professional development.

- Reflect on your experiences and use them as opportunities for learning and growth.

6. Set Flexible Goals:

- Set clear, achievable goals that align with your values and aspirations. Be prepared to adjust your goals in response to changing circumstances and new opportunities.

- Regularly review and update your goals to ensure they remain relevant and motivating.

7. Embrace Change:

- Develop a positive attitude toward change by viewing it as a natural and necessary part of life. Focus on the potential benefits and opportunities that change can bring.

- Practice mindfulness to stay present and manage stress during times of change.

8. Seek Diverse Experiences:

- Expose yourself to new environments, cultures, and activities to broaden your horizons and develop greater adaptability.

- Engage with people from different backgrounds and perspectives to enhance your understanding and empathy.

Real-Life Examples of Adaptability

1. Sheryl Sandberg: Navigating Personal and Professional Challenges

- Sheryl Sandberg, COO of Facebook and author of "Lean In," demonstrated adaptability in the face of personal tragedy and professional challenges. After the sudden death of her husband, Sandberg embraced change by seeking support, building resilience, and focusing on her family's well-being. Professionally, she navigated the dynamic tech industry by continuously learning and adapting to new trends and challenges.

2. Elon Musk: Pioneering Innovator

- Elon Musk, founder of Tesla and SpaceX, exemplifies adaptability through his willingness to take risks and embrace change. Musk's ability to pivot between industries, from electric vehicles to space exploration, demonstrates his flexibility and openness to new ideas. His commitment to continuous learning and innovation has enabled him to achieve groundbreaking success in multiple fields.

3. Malala Yousafzai: Advocacy for Education

- Malala Yousafzai's adaptability is evident in her resilience and determination to advocate for girls' education despite facing life-threatening adversity. After surviving an assassination attempt by the Taliban, Malala continued her activism on a global scale, adapting her strategies to reach a wider audience and influence policy changes. Her ability to embrace change and remain committed to her cause has made her a powerful symbol of courage and resilience.

Practical Exercises for Developing Adaptability

1. Change Your Routine:

- Experiment with changing your daily routine to introduce new experiences and develop flexibility. Try new activities, explore different environments, and engage with diverse groups of people.

2. Set Stretch Goals:

- Challenge yourself by setting stretch goals that push you beyond your comfort zone. These goals should be ambitious yet achievable, motivating you to adapt and grow.

3. Engage in Reflective Practices:

- Incorporate reflective practices, such as journaling or meditation, into your daily routine to enhance self-awareness and track your growth. Reflect on your experiences, emotions, and lessons learned to gain insights and identify areas for improvement.

4. Develop a Personal Adaptability Plan:

- Create a personal adaptability plan that outlines your goals, strategies, and timeline for developing greater flexibility and openness to change. Review and update your plan regularly to stay on track and adjust to new interests.

Adaptability is a crucial skill for personal growth, professional success, and overall well-being. By cultivating a growth mindset, staying curious and open-minded, practicing flexibility, building resilience, and engaging in continuous learning, we can develop greater adaptability and thrive in an ever-changing world. Real-life examples of individuals who have embraced change, like Sheryl Sandberg, Elon Musk, and Malala Yousafzai, inspire us to prioritize adaptability and strive for continuous improvement. As we continue exploring the Law of Growth, let these strategies and practices guide us toward a more dynamic, resilient, and fulfilling life, where adaptability becomes a key driver of our success and well-being.

Goal Setting: Methods for Setting and Achieving Personal and Professional Goals

Setting and achieving goals is a fundamental aspect of personal and professional growth. Goals provide direction, motivation, and a sense of purpose, helping us focus our efforts and make meaningful progress in our lives. This chapter explores effective methods for setting and achieving goals, emphasizing the importance of clarity, planning, and persistence.

The Importance of Goal Setting

Goal setting is a powerful tool for personal and professional development. It helps us:

1. Clarify Our Vision: Goals provide a clear sense of direction and purpose, helping us define what we want to achieve.

2. Enhance Motivation: Setting goals motivates us to take action and stay committed to our objectives.

3. Improve Focus: Goals help us prioritize our time and resources, ensuring that we concentrate on activities that contribute to our desired outcomes.

4. Measure Progress: Setting specific goals allows us to track our progress and celebrate our achievements.

Key Principles of Effective Goal Setting

To set and achieve meaningful goals, consider the following principles:

1. Specificity: Clearly define your goals with specific details. Vague goals are difficult to achieve because they lack direction.

2. Measurability: Ensure that your goals are measurable so you can track your progress and determine when you have achieved them.

3. Achievability: Set realistic and attainable goals that are challenging yet within your capabilities.

4. Relevance: Align your goals with your values, priorities, and long-term vision to ensure they are meaningful and motivating.

5. Time-Bound: Establish deadlines for your goals to create a sense of urgency and maintain momentum.

Methods for Setting and Achieving Goals

1. SMART Goals:

- The SMART framework is a widely used method for setting effective goals. SMART stands for Specific, Measurable, Achievable, Relevant, and Time-Bound.

- Specific: Clearly define what you want to achieve. For example, "Increase sales by 20% within the next six months."

- Measurable: Identify indicators to track your progress. For example, "Track monthly sales reports."

- Achievable: Set realistic goals that are challenging but attainable. For example, "Implement a new marketing strategy to reach potential customers."

- Relevant: Ensure your goals align with your overall objectives. For example, "Increase sales to support business growth."

- Time-Bound: Establish a deadline to achieve your goals. For example, "Achieve a 20% increase in sales by June 30."

2. Chunking:

- Break down large goals into smaller, manageable tasks. This approach, known as chunking, makes goals less overwhelming and easier to achieve.

- Create a step-by-step plan outlining the tasks and milestones required to achieve your goal. Focus on completing one task at a time to maintain momentum.

3. Visualization:

- Use visualization techniques to imagine yourself achieving your goals. Visualization helps reinforce your commitment and motivates you to take action.

- Spend a few minutes each day visualizing the successful completion of your goals and experiencing the positive emotions associated with your achievements.

4. Accountability:

- Share your goals with others to increase accountability. Discuss your progress with a trusted friend, mentor, or accountability partner who can provide support and encouragement.

- Regularly update your accountability partner on your progress and seek feedback and advice when needed.

5. Action Plans:

- Develop a detailed action plan outlining the steps required to achieve your goals. Include specific tasks, deadlines, and resources needed for each step.

- Review and update your action plan regularly to stay on track and make adjustments as needed.

6. Tracking Progress:

- Use tools such as journals, spreadsheets, or goal-tracking apps to monitor your progress. Regularly review your progress and celebrate small achievements along the way.

- Adjust your approach if you encounter obstacles or setbacks, and stay committed to your goals.

7. Flexibility:

- Be flexible and open to adjusting your goals as circumstances change. If you encounter unforeseen challenges or new opportunities, reassess your goals and make necessary modifications.

- Maintain a positive attitude and view setbacks as learning experiences that can inform your future efforts.

Real-Life Examples of Goal Setting

1. J.K. Rowling: Achieving Literary Success

- J.K. Rowling, the author of the Harry Potter series, faced numerous rejections before achieving literary success. She set clear goals for her writing and remained committed despite facing significant challenges, including financial difficulties and personal struggles. Her persistence and dedication to her goals led to the creation of one of the most successful book series in history.

2. Elon Musk: Transforming Industries

- Elon Musk, the entrepreneur behind companies like Tesla and SpaceX, is known for setting ambitious and transformative goals. Musk's vision of advancing sustainable energy and space exploration drives his goal-setting approach. By breaking down his grand vision into achievable milestones, Musk has successfully launched electric vehicles, reusable rockets, and solar energy products, revolutionizing multiple industries.

3. Serena Williams: Athletic Excellence

- Serena Williams, one of the greatest tennis players of all time, exemplifies the power of goal setting in achieving athletic excellence. Williams sets specific goals for her training, performance, and tournaments, and works diligently to achieve them. Her focus, discipline, and commitment to her goals have earned her numerous titles and accolades in the world of tennis.

Practical Exercises for Goal Setting

1. Goal-Setting Worksheet:

- Create a goal-setting worksheet that outlines your SMART goals, action steps, deadlines, and progress tracking. Use this worksheet to organize and monitor your goals regularly.

2. Weekly Goal Review:

- Set aside time each week to review your goals and assess your progress. Reflect on your achievements, identify any obstacles, and plan your next steps. Use this time to celebrate your successes and make adjustments as needed.

3. Vision Board:

- Create a vision board that visually represents your goals and aspirations. Include images, quotes, and symbols that inspire and motivate you. Place your vision board in a prominent location where you can see it daily.

4. Accountability Partner:

- Find an accountability partner with whom you can share your goals and progress. Schedule regular check-ins to discuss your achievements, challenges, and next steps. Offer support and encouragement to each other.

5. Goal Journal:

- Keep a goal journal to document your goals, action plans, progress, and reflections. Use your journal to track your achievements, learn from your experiences, and stay motivated.

Goal setting is a powerful tool for personal and professional growth. By setting clear, specific, and achievable goals, we can enhance our motivation, focus, and sense of purpose. Effective goal-setting methods, such as the SMART framework, chunking, visualization, accountability, and action planning, help us stay on track and achieve our objectives. Real-life examples of successful individuals, like J.K. Rowling, Elon Musk, and Serena Williams, demonstrate the transformative power of goal setting. As we continue exploring the Law of Growth, let these strategies and practices guide us toward a more intentional, goal-oriented, and fulfilling life, where our aspirations become tangible achievements.

Real-Life Examples: Inspirational Stories of Individuals Who Have Embraced Growth and Transformation

Personal growth and transformation often arise from the ability to embrace change, set goals, and continuously seek improvement. The following real-life examples highlight individuals who have overcome significant challenges and achieved remarkable success by embracing the Law of Growth.

1. Oprah Winfrey: From Poverty to Media Mogul
Background:

Oprah Winfrey's journey from a challenging childhood to becoming one of the most influential women in the world is a testament to the power of personal growth and transformation. Born into poverty in rural Mississippi, Winfrey faced numerous hardships, including abuse and discrimination.

Growth and Transformation:

Despite her difficult upbringing, Winfrey's determination to succeed never wavered. She embraced education as a path to a better life, earning a full scholarship to Tennessee State University. Winfrey's career in media began with a local radio station, which eventually led to her hosting a morning talk show in Chicago. Her ability to connect with audiences and her authentic, empathetic approach quickly garnered attention.

Remarkable Success:

Winfrey's talk show, "The Oprah Winfrey Show," became the highest-rated television talk show in history, running for 25 years. She founded Harpo Productions, launched her own television network (OWN), and became a prominent philanthropist. Winfrey's commitment to personal growth, education, and empowerment has inspired millions worldwide, showcasing the transformative power of embracing change and setting ambitious goals.

2. Nelson Mandela: From Prisoner to President

Background:

Nelson Mandela, a South African anti-apartheid revolutionary, spent 27 years in prison for his activism against the oppressive apartheid regime. His journey is a powerful example of resilience, personal growth, and the pursuit of justice.

Growth and Transformation:

During his imprisonment, Mandela remained committed to his vision of a free and equal South Africa. He used his time in prison for self-reflection, education, and developing a deeper understanding of leadership and reconciliation. Mandela's unwavering belief in justice and equality fueled his determination to overcome the immense challenges he faced.

Remarkable Success:

After his release from prison in 1990, Mandela continued his activism, playing a crucial role in the negotiations that led to the end of apartheid. In 1994, he became South Africa's first black president, leading the country through a transformative period of reconciliation and nation-building. Mandela's legacy of forgiveness, leadership, and dedication to human rights continues to inspire generations globally.

3. J.K. Rowling: From Struggling Writer to Literary Icon

Background:

J.K. Rowling, the author of the Harry Potter series, faced significant personal and professional challenges before achieving literary success. As a single mother living on welfare, Rowling struggled to make ends meet while pursuing her dream of becoming a writer.

Growth and Transformation:

Despite numerous rejections from publishers, Rowling's belief in her story and her dedication to her craft never waned. She continued to write and refine her manuscript, driven by her passion for storytelling and her desire to provide a better life for her daughter.

Remarkable Success:

Rowling's perseverance paid off when Bloomsbury Publishing accepted her manuscript for publication. The Harry Potter series became a global phenomenon, selling over 500 million copies and being adapted into a successful film franchise. Rowling's journey from struggling writer to literary icon underscores the importance of resilience, self-belief, and continuous growth.

4. Elon Musk: Innovator and Entrepreneur

Background:

Elon Musk, the entrepreneur behind companies like Tesla, SpaceX, and SolarCity, has faced numerous obstacles and setbacks on his path to success. His vision for advancing technology and sustainability has driven his relentless pursuit of innovation.

Growth and Transformation:

Musk's journey is marked by his ability to embrace failure as a learning opportunity and his willingness to take bold risks. Despite early failures with SpaceX, including multiple rocket launch failures, Musk remained committed to his vision of making space travel more accessible and affordable. Similarly, Tesla faced significant financial challenges and skepticism from the automotive industry.

Remarkable Success:

Musk's persistence and innovative approach led to groundbreaking achievements. SpaceX became the first privately-funded company to send a spacecraft to the International Space Station, revolutionizing space travel. Tesla has transformed the automotive industry with its electric vehicles, leading the transition to sustainable energy. Musk's ability to embrace growth and transformation has made him one of the most influential innovators of our time.

5. Malala Yousafzai: Advocate for Girls' Education

Background:

Malala Yousafzai, a Pakistani education activist, faced life-threatening adversity in her fight for girls' education. At the age of 15, she survived an assassination attempt by the Taliban, who opposed her advocacy for education.

Growth and Transformation:

Despite the attack, Malala's commitment to education and equality only grew stronger. She continued her activism on a global scale, using her platform to raise awareness about the importance of education for girls and speaking out against oppression and violence.

Remarkable Success:

Malala's efforts have been recognized worldwide. In 2014, she became the youngest recipient of the Nobel Peace Prize. She founded the Malala Fund, which supports education initiatives for girls in various countries. Malala's resilience and dedication to her cause exemplify the power of embracing growth and transformation in the face of adversity.

These real-life examples illustrate the transformative power of embracing growth and change. By setting ambitious goals, remaining resilient in the face of challenges, and continuously seeking improvement, individuals like Oprah Winfrey, Nelson Mandela, J.K. Rowling, Elon Musk, and Malala Yousafzai have achieved remarkable success and made significant contributions to the world. Their stories inspire us to embrace the Law of Growth, pursue our dreams with determination, and view challenges as opportunities for personal and professional development. As we continue exploring the Law of Growth, let these examples guide and motivate us on our journey toward a more fulfilling and impactful life.

CHAPTER 04

THE LAW OF RESPONSIBILITY

Owning Your Life

The Law of Responsibility asserts that we are the architects of our own lives. It emphasizes the importance of taking ownership of our actions, decisions, and circumstances. By embracing this law, we empower ourselves to create the life we desire, recognizing that our choices and attitudes shape our reality. This chapter explores the principles of personal responsibility, the benefits of owning our lives, and practical strategies for taking charge of our destiny.

Understanding Personal Responsibility

Personal responsibility means recognizing that we have control over our actions and their outcomes. It involves accepting that we are accountable for our decisions and behaviors, rather than blaming external factors or other people. By taking ownership of our lives, we acknowledge our role in shaping our experiences and outcomes.

Key Principles of Personal Responsibility:

1. Accountability: Accepting responsibility for our actions and their consequences, both positive and negative.

2. Self-Empowerment: Recognizing that we have the power to influence our lives through our choices and actions.

3. Proactivity: Taking initiative to create the life we desire, rather than waiting for circumstances to change.

4. Integrity: Acting in alignment with our values and principles, and being honest with ourselves and others.

The Importance of Owning Your Life

Owning our lives is crucial for several reasons:

1. Empowerment: Taking responsibility for our actions empowers us to make positive changes and take control of our destiny.

2. Self-Respect: When we own our lives, we build self-respect and confidence in our ability to navigate challenges and achieve our goals.

3. Growth and Learning: Accepting responsibility for our mistakes and failures allows us to learn from them and grow as individuals.

4. Positive Relationships: Personal responsibility fosters trust and respect in our relationships, as others recognize our integrity and reliability.

5. Fulfillment: By taking charge of our lives, we create a sense of purpose and fulfillment, knowing that we are actively shaping our own path.

Strategies for Owning Your Life

To take ownership of your life, consider the following strategies:

1. Set Clear Goals:

   - Define clear, achievable goals that align with your values and aspirations. Break these goals into smaller, manageable steps to make them more attainable.

   - Regularly review and adjust your goals to reflect your evolving interests and circumstances.

2. Take Initiative:

   - Be proactive in pursuing your goals and addressing challenges. Take the first step, even when it feels daunting, and maintain momentum by consistently taking action.

   - Avoid waiting for external factors to change; focus on what you can control and influence.

3. Embrace Accountability:

- Hold yourself accountable for your actions and their outcomes. If you make a mistake, acknowledge it, learn from it, and take steps to make amends.

- Seek feedback from others and use it to improve your behavior and decision-making.

4. Practice Self-Reflection:

- Regularly reflect on your actions, decisions, and their consequences. Use journaling or meditation to enhance self-awareness and gain insights into your behavior.

- Identify patterns in your behavior and areas for improvement, and commit to making positive changes.

5. Develop a Positive Mindset:

- Cultivate a positive attitude by focusing on opportunities and solutions rather than problems. Practice gratitude and appreciation for the positive aspects of your life.

- Challenge self-limiting beliefs and replace them with empowering affirmations that reinforce your ability to create the life you desire.

6. Take Responsibility for Your Emotions:

- Recognize that you have control over your emotional responses. Practice emotional intelligence by managing your emotions and responding thoughtfully to challenging situations.

- Use mindfulness techniques to stay present and maintain emotional balance.

7. Build Resilience:

- Strengthen your resilience by developing coping strategies for dealing with stress and adversity. Maintain a positive outlook and focus on your strengths and resources.

- View setbacks as opportunities for growth and learning, and use them to build resilience and perseverance.

8. Seek Personal Growth:

- Commit to continuous learning and self-improvement. Seek new knowledge, skills, and experiences that align with your goals and values.

- Surround yourself with positive influences, including supportive friends, mentors, and role models who encourage your growth.

Real-Life Examples of Owning Your Life

1. Viktor Frankl: Finding Meaning in Adversity

- Viktor Frankl, a Holocaust survivor and psychiatrist, demonstrated profound personal responsibility by finding meaning in the most challenging circumstances. Despite enduring immense suffering in concentration camps, Frankl maintained a sense of purpose and dignity. He later developed logotherapy, a therapeutic approach that emphasizes finding meaning in life. Frankl's story illustrates the power of owning one's life, even in the face of extreme adversity.

2. Maya Angelou: Overcoming Trauma and Empowering Others

- Maya Angelou, a renowned poet and civil rights activist, overcame significant personal trauma and adversity to become a powerful voice for change. Throughout her life, Angelou took responsibility for her actions and choices, using her experiences to inspire and empower others. Her resilience, self-awareness, and commitment to personal growth are testament to the transformative power of owning one's life.

3. Stephen Hawking: Defying Physical Limitations

- Despite being diagnosed with a debilitating motor neuron disease at a young age, Stephen Hawking took responsibility for his life and made significant contributions to the field of theoretical physics. Hawking's determination to pursue his passion for science and his refusal to be defined by his physical limitations exemplify the importance of personal responsibility in achieving one's goals and making a meaningful impact.

Practical Exercises for Owning Your Life

1. Personal Responsibility Audit:

- Conduct a personal responsibility audit by reviewing various aspects of your life, including your goals, relationships, and daily habits. Identify areas where you can take more responsibility and make positive changes.

2. Action Plan:

- Create an action plan that outlines specific steps you will take to own your life. Include short-term and long-term goals, along with actionable tasks and deadlines. Regularly review and update your plan to stay on track.

3. Daily Reflection:

- Set aside time each day for reflection. Consider your actions, decisions, and their outcomes. Reflect on what you have learned and how you can apply these insights to improve your life.

4. Accountability Partner:

- Find an accountability partner with whom you can share your goals and progress. Schedule regular check-ins to discuss your achievements, challenges, and next steps. Offer support and encouragement to each other.

5. Affirmations:

- Use positive affirmations to reinforce your commitment to personal responsibility. Create affirmations that resonate with your goals and values, and repeat them daily to cultivate a positive mindset.

The Law of Responsibility empowers us to take ownership of our actions, decisions, and circumstances. By embracing personal responsibility, we can shape our lives according to our values and aspirations, creating a sense of purpose and fulfillment. Strategies such as setting clear goals, taking initiative, embracing accountability, and practicing self-reflection can help us take charge of our destiny. Real-life examples of individuals who have owned their lives, like Viktor Frankl, Maya Angelou, and Stephen Hawking, inspire us to embrace this powerful principle and strive for continuous growth and improvement. As we continue exploring the Law of Responsibility, let these strategies and practices guide us toward a more empowered, intentional, and fulfilling life, where we are the architects of our own destiny.

Empowerment Practices: Self-Reflection

Self-reflection is a powerful tool for gaining insight into one's actions, decisions, and overall life journey. It involves taking a step back to examine our thoughts, behaviors, and experiences to understand ourselves better and make informed decisions. This chapter explores the importance of self-reflection, its benefits, and practical techniques for incorporating this practice into our daily lives to foster personal empowerment and growth.

Understanding Self-Reflection

Self-reflection is the process of introspection, where we consciously evaluate our thoughts, feelings, actions, and their outcomes. It allows us to identify patterns, recognize areas for improvement, and celebrate our successes. By engaging in regular self-reflection, we develop greater self-awareness, which is crucial for personal development and responsible decision-making.

Key Aspects of Self-Reflection:

1. Introspection: Looking inward to examine our thoughts, emotions, and motivations.

2. Evaluation: Assessing our actions and decisions to understand their impact.

3. Learning: Identifying lessons from our experiences to inform future behavior.

4. Growth: Using insights gained from self-reflection to foster personal development.

The Importance of Self-Reflection

Self-reflection is essential for several reasons:

1. Enhanced Self-Awareness: Understanding our strengths, weaknesses, and motivations helps us make better decisions and align our actions with our values.

2. Personal Growth: Reflecting on our experiences allows us to learn from them, fostering continuous improvement and development.

3. Improved Relationships: By understanding our behavior and its impact on others, we can cultivate healthier, more empathetic relationships.

4. Informed Decision-Making: Self-reflection provides clarity, helping us make more thoughtful and deliberate choices.

5. Emotional Regulation: Reflecting on our emotions and reactions enables us to manage them more effectively, promoting emotional well-being.

Techniques for Self-Reflection

To incorporate self-reflection into your daily routine, consider the following techniques:

1. Journaling:

   - Writing in a journal is one of the most effective ways to engage in self-reflection. Document your thoughts, feelings, and experiences regularly.

   - Use prompts to guide your journaling, such as "What did I learn today?" or "How did I handle a challenging situation?"

2. Meditation:

- Practice mindfulness meditation to cultivate a state of present-moment awareness. Focus on your breath and observe your thoughts and feelings without judgment.

- Use guided meditations that encourage self-reflection and introspection.

3. Daily Reflection:

- Set aside time each day for reflection. Consider what went well, what challenges you faced, and what you learned.

- Reflect on specific events or interactions and analyze your responses and their outcomes.

4. Self-Assessment:

- Use self-assessment tools and questionnaires to evaluate your behavior, attitudes, and progress toward your goals.

- Regularly assess your strengths and areas for improvement to inform your personal development plan.

5. Feedback Seeking:

- Seek feedback from trusted friends, family members, or colleagues. Use their insights to gain a different perspective on your actions and decisions.

- Reflect on the feedback received and consider how you can apply it to improve.

6. Mind Mapping:

- Create mind maps to visually organize your thoughts and ideas. This technique can help you explore different aspects of your experiences and identify connections between them.

- Use mind maps to brainstorm solutions to challenges or plan for future goals.

7. Reflective Reading:

- Read books, articles, and other resources that encourage self-reflection and personal growth. Reflect on how the content relates to your own experiences and insights.

- Keep a reading journal to document your thoughts and takeaways from your reading materials.

Practical Exercises for Self-Reflection

1. Weekly Review:

- At the end of each week, review your actions, decisions, and experiences. Identify key lessons learned and areas for improvement.

- Use a structured format, such as a weekly review template, to organize your reflections and set intentions for the upcoming week.

2. SWOT Analysis:

- Conduct a personal SWOT analysis to identify your strengths, weaknesses, opportunities, and threats.

Reflect on how you can leverage your strengths and opportunities while addressing your weaknesses and threats.

- Update your SWOT analysis regularly to track your progress and adapt to changing circumstances.

3. Gratitude Journal:

- Keep a gratitude journal to document things you are grateful for each day. Reflecting on positive experiences can enhance your overall well-being and promote a positive mindset.

- Use your gratitude journal to identify patterns of positivity and areas where you can cultivate more gratitude in your life.

4. Reflective Questions:

- Use reflective questions to guide your introspection. Some examples include:

- What were my biggest accomplishments this week/month/year?

- How did I handle challenges or setbacks?

- What am I most proud of?

- What do I want to improve or change moving forward?

- Answer these questions regularly to gain deeper insights into your personal growth and development.

5. Vision Board:

- Create a vision board that visually represents your goals, aspirations, and values. Use it as a tool for self-reflection and motivation.

- Regularly review your vision board to reflect on your progress and make adjustments as needed.

Real-Life Examples of Self-Reflection

1. Mahatma Gandhi: The Power of Introspection

- Mahatma Gandhi, a leader of the Indian independence movement, was known for his practice of self-reflection and introspection. Gandhi regularly engaged in self-examination to align his actions with his principles of nonviolence and truth. His commitment to self-reflection helped him lead a life of integrity and inspire millions worldwide.

2. Oprah Winfrey: Journaling for Self-Discovery

- Oprah Winfrey, a media mogul and philanthropist, has long advocated for the practice of journaling. Winfrey attributes much of her personal growth and success to her regular journaling habit, which allows her to reflect on her experiences, set intentions, and gain clarity on her goals. Her practice of self-reflection has been instrumental in her journey of empowerment and transformation.

3. Nelson Mandela: Reflective Leadership

- Nelson Mandela, the former president of South Africa, utilized self-reflection during his 27 years of imprisonment. Mandela reflected on his actions, beliefs, and the future of his country. His practice of introspection helped him develop the resilience and vision needed to lead South Africa through a peaceful transition from apartheid to democracy.

Self-reflection is a powerful empowerment practice that fosters self-awareness, personal growth, and responsible decision-making. By incorporating techniques such as journaling, meditation, daily reflection, and feedback seeking into our daily routine, we can gain deeper insights into our actions and decisions. Real-life examples of individuals who have embraced self-reflection, like Mahatma Gandhi, Oprah Winfrey, and Nelson Mandela, demonstrate the transformative power of this practice. As we continue exploring the Law of Responsibility, let these strategies for self-reflection guide us toward a more empowered, intentional, and fulfilling life, where we take ownership of our actions and strive for continuous growth and improvement.

Accountability: Building a Network of Support and Accountability

Accountability is a crucial aspect of personal and professional growth. It involves taking responsibility for our actions, decisions, and commitments while leveraging a network of support to help us stay on track. Building a network of support and accountability can significantly enhance our ability to achieve our goals and foster meaningful connections with others. This chapter explores the importance of accountability, the benefits of having an accountability network, and practical strategies for building and maintaining such a network.

Understanding Accountability

Accountability means being answerable for our actions and decisions. It involves recognizing our responsibilities and being willing to explain our actions to ourselves and others. Accountability helps ensure that we follow through on our commitments and strive to achieve our goals.

Key Components of Accountability:

1. Responsibility: Acknowledging our duties and the impact of our actions.

2. Commitment: Dedication to following through on our goals and promises.

3. Transparency: Being open and honest about our progress, challenges, and decisions.

4. Support: Seeking and providing encouragement, feedback, and assistance from others.

The Importance of Accountability

Accountability is essential for several reasons:

1. Enhanced Motivation: Knowing that we are accountable to others increases our motivation to achieve our goals.

2. Improved Performance: Accountability helps us stay focused, disciplined, and committed to our objectives.

3. Personal Growth: Being accountable encourages us to reflect on our actions, learn from our experiences, and continuously improve.

4. Stronger Relationships: Accountability fosters trust and mutual respect in our relationships, as it demonstrates reliability and integrity.

5. Achievement of Goals: With accountability, we are more likely to set realistic goals, develop effective plans, and achieve our desired outcomes.

Building a Network of Support and Accountability

To build a network of support and accountability, consider the following strategies:

1. Identify Accountability Partners:

- Choose individuals who share similar goals, values, and levels of commitment. These can be friends, family members, colleagues, or mentors.

- Look for partners who are reliable, supportive, and willing to provide honest feedback.

2. Set Clear Expectations:

- Define the roles and responsibilities of each accountability partner. Clarify what you expect from each other in terms of support, feedback, and check-ins.

- Establish guidelines for how often you will communicate and how you will track progress.

3. Create Accountability Agreements:

- Formalize your commitment to each other by creating written accountability agreements. Outline your goals, action plans, and timelines.

- Include specific details about how you will hold each other accountable and the consequences of not meeting commitments.

4. Regular Check-Ins:

- Schedule regular check-ins to discuss progress, challenges, and next steps. These can be weekly, bi-weekly, or monthly, depending on your needs and goals.

- Use check-ins to celebrate successes, address obstacles, and provide encouragement and feedback.

5. Provide Constructive Feedback:

- Offer honest and constructive feedback to your accountability partners. Focus on providing specific, actionable suggestions for improvement.

- Be open to receiving feedback from your partners and use it to enhance your performance and achieve your goals.

6. Celebrate Achievements:

- Recognize and celebrate each other's achievements, no matter how small. Celebrating successes reinforces positive behavior and boosts motivation.

- Use milestones and rewards to mark significant progress and maintain momentum.

7. Stay Flexible and Adaptable:

- Be willing to adjust your accountability plans as needed. If circumstances change or new challenges arise, reassess your goals and strategies.

- Maintain open communication with your accountability partners to ensure that your support network remains effective and relevant.

8. Use Technology:

- Leverage technology to facilitate communication and track progress. Use tools such as goal-tracking apps, project management software, and video conferencing platforms.

- Create shared documents or online workspaces where you can collaborate and monitor each other's progress.

Real-Life Examples of Accountability Networks

1. Professional Peer Groups:

- Many successful professionals participate in peer groups or mastermind groups where they share goals, challenges, and strategies. These groups provide a supportive environment for accountability, feedback, and collaboration.

- For example, CEOs often join executive peer groups where they discuss business challenges, set goals, and hold each other accountable for their commitments.

2. Fitness Accountability Partners:

- Fitness enthusiasts often pair up with workout partners to stay motivated and committed to their fitness goals. These partners provide encouragement, share progress, and hold each other accountable for sticking to their exercise routines.

- For instance, training for a marathon with a running partner can significantly increase the likelihood of completing the training program and achieving the goal.

3. Writing Accountability Groups:

- Writers and authors frequently join writing groups or find accountability partners to stay disciplined and productive. These groups provide deadlines, feedback, and motivation to help writers complete their projects.

- For example, NaNoWriMo (National Novel Writing Month) participants often form accountability groups to support each other in reaching the goal of writing a 50,000-word novel in one month.

4. Educational Study Groups:

- Students often form study groups to enhance their learning experience and stay accountable for their academic goals. These groups encourage regular study sessions, share resources, and provide mutual support.

- For instance, medical students preparing for board exams may form study groups to review materials, quiz each other, and stay motivated during intensive study periods.

Practical Exercises for Building Accountability

1. Accountability Partner Selection:

- Identify potential accountability partners who share your goals and values. Reach out to them and discuss the possibility of forming an accountability partnership.

- Evaluate the compatibility and commitment levels of potential partners before formalizing the partnership.

2. Accountability Agreement Creation:

- Draft an accountability agreement that outlines your goals, action plans, timelines, and check-in schedules. Share this agreement with your accountability partners and review it together.

- Ensure that the agreement is clear, specific, and mutually agreed upon.

3. Weekly Accountability Check-Ins:

- Schedule weekly check-ins with your accountability partners to discuss your progress, challenges, and next steps. Use these check-ins to provide feedback and encouragement.

- Keep a record of your check-ins and track your progress over time.

4. Feedback and Reflection:

- Practice giving and receiving constructive feedback with your accountability partners. Focus on providing specific, actionable suggestions for improvement.

- Reflect on the feedback you receive and use it to adjust your goals and strategies.

5. Celebration of Achievements:

- Plan regular celebrations or rewards for achieving milestones and goals. Share your achievements with your accountability partners and celebrate together.

- Use celebrations to reinforce positive behavior and maintain motivation.

Accountability is a powerful tool for personal and professional growth. By building a network of support and accountability, we can enhance our motivation, improve our performance, and achieve our goals. Strategies such as identifying accountability partners, setting clear expectations, creating accountability agreements, and providing constructive feedback can help us build and maintain effective accountability networks. Real-life examples of accountability networks, such as professional peer groups, fitness partners, writing groups, and study groups, demonstrate the benefits of this approach. As we continue exploring the Law of Responsibility, let these strategies guide us toward a more empowered, intentional, and fulfilling life, where accountability becomes a key driver of our success and well-being.

Proactive Living: Strategies for Taking Control of One's Life and Destiny

Proactive living is about taking charge of our lives, making intentional choices, and actively pursuing our goals. It involves anticipating challenges, planning ahead, and taking decisive actions to shape our future. By embracing a proactive mindset, we can transform our lives and achieve our aspirations. This chapter explores the principles of proactive living, its benefits, and practical strategies for taking control of one's life and destiny.

Understanding Proactive Living

Proactive living means taking responsibility for our actions and decisions rather than reacting passively to events and circumstances. It involves being intentional, setting clear goals, and taking consistent action to achieve those goals. Proactive individuals focus on what they can control and influence, rather than dwelling on external factors beyond their control.

Key Principles of Proactive Living:

1. Intentionality: Making deliberate choices aligned with our values and goals.

2. Responsibility: Accepting ownership of our actions and their outcomes.

3. Planning: Anticipating challenges and opportunities, and preparing accordingly.

4. Action: Taking consistent, purposeful steps to achieve our objectives.

5. Resilience: Adapting to setbacks and persisting in the face of challenges.

The Importance of Proactive Living

Proactive living is essential for several reasons:

1. Empowerment: Taking control of our lives empowers us to create the future we desire.

2. Achievement: Proactive individuals are more likely to achieve their goals and aspirations.

3. Resilience: Being proactive helps us anticipate and navigate challenges, reducing stress and uncertainty.

4. Fulfillment: Living intentionally and achieving our goals leads to a greater sense of fulfillment and purpose.

5. Positive Impact: Proactive individuals can influence their environment and inspire others to take charge of their lives.

Strategies for Proactive Living

To cultivate a proactive mindset and take control of your life and destiny, consider the following strategies:

1. Set Clear Goals:

- Define specific, achievable goals that align with your values and aspirations. Break these goals into smaller, manageable steps to make them more attainable.

- Regularly review and adjust your goals to reflect your evolving interests and circumstances.

2. Develop a Vision:

- Create a clear vision of what you want your life to look like. Visualize your ideal future in detail, considering all aspects of your life, including career, relationships, health, and personal growth.

- Use your vision as a guiding star to stay focused and motivated.

3. Create Action Plans:

- Develop detailed action plans outlining the steps required to achieve your goals. Include specific tasks, deadlines, and resources needed for each step.

- Review and update your action plans regularly to stay on track and make adjustments as needed.

4. Prioritize Your Time:

- Identify your most important tasks and prioritize them in your daily schedule. Focus on high-impact activities that contribute directly to your goals.

- Use time management techniques, such as the Eisenhower Matrix or time blocking, to stay organized and productive.

5. Take Initiative:

- Be proactive in pursuing your goals and addressing challenges. Take the first step, even when it feels daunting, and maintain momentum by consistently taking action.

- Avoid waiting for external factors to change; focus on what you can control and influence.

6. Build Resilience:

- Strengthen your resilience by developing coping strategies for dealing with stress and adversity. Maintain a positive attitude and focus on your strengths and resources.

- View setbacks as opportunities for growth and learning, and use them to build resilience and perseverance.

7. Seek Feedback and Support:

- Seek feedback from trusted friends, family members, or mentors. Use their insights to gain a different perspective on your actions and decisions.

- Surround yourself with a supportive network of individuals who encourage your growth and provide accountability.

8. Reflect and Adjust:

- Regularly reflect on your progress and experiences. Assess what is working well and what needs improvement.

- Use self-reflection to make informed adjustments to your goals, plans, and strategies.

Real-Life Examples of Proactive Living

1. Steve Jobs: Visionary Leadership

- Steve Jobs, co-founder of Apple Inc., exemplified proactive living through his visionary leadership and relentless pursuit of innovation. Jobs had a clear vision for Apple and took decisive actions to transform the company into a global leader in technology. His proactive approach to design, marketing, and business strategy revolutionized multiple industries and left a lasting legacy.

2. Marie Curie: Pioneering Scientist

- Marie Curie, a pioneering physicist and chemist, demonstrated proactive living by taking control of her scientific career despite facing significant obstacles. Curie's intentional pursuit of research on radioactivity led to groundbreaking discoveries, including the elements polonium and radium. Her proactive approach to scientific inquiry earned her two Nobel Prizes and advanced the field of science.

3. Malala Yousafzai: Education Advocate

- Malala Yousafzai's proactive advocacy for girls' education showcases the power of taking control of one's destiny. Despite facing life-threatening adversity, Malala continued her activism on a global scale, using her platform to raise awareness and drive change. Her proactive efforts have resulted in increased access to education for girls worldwide and inspired countless individuals to take action for social justice.

Practical Exercises for Proactive Living

1. Vision Board:

- Create a vision board that visually represents your goals, aspirations, and values. Include images, quotes, and symbols that inspire and motivate you.

- Place your vision board in a prominent location where you can see it daily to stay focused on your goals.

2. Weekly Planning Session:

- Set aside time each week to plan your upcoming tasks and activities. Review your goals and action plans, and prioritize your most important tasks.

- Use this time to reflect on your progress, celebrate successes, and make any necessary adjustments.

3. Goal Setting Worksheet:

- Use a goal-setting worksheet to define your goals, outline action steps, and set deadlines. Track your progress and update the worksheet regularly.

- Share your goals and progress with an accountability partner to stay motivated and committed.

4. Daily Reflection Journal:

- Keep a daily reflection journal to document your thoughts, experiences, and insights. Reflect on what went well, what challenges you faced, and what you learned.

- Use your journal to identify patterns, set intentions, and make informed decisions.

5. Time Management Techniques:

- Experiment with different time management techniques, such as the Pomodoro Technique, time blocking, or the Eisenhower Matrix, to find what works best for you.

- Implement these techniques in your daily routine to stay organized and productive.

Proactive living is about taking control of our lives, making intentional choices, and actively pursuing our goals. By setting clear goals, developing a vision, creating action plans, and building resilience, we can shape our destiny and achieve our aspirations. Strategies such as prioritizing time, seeking feedback and support, and reflecting and adjusting our approach help us stay focused and motivated. Real-life examples of proactive individuals, like Steve Jobs, Marie Curie, and Malala Yousafzai, inspire us to embrace a proactive mindset and take charge of our lives. As we continue exploring the Law of Responsibility, let these strategies guide us toward a more empowered, intentional, and fulfilling life, where we actively create the future we desire.

Real-Life Examples: Transforming Challenges into Opportunities for Growth and Success

Taking responsibility for one's life involves recognizing and accepting the power of personal choice and action in shaping one's destiny. Many individuals have faced significant challenges yet have transformed these obstacles into opportunities for growth and success by taking full responsibility for their lives. This chapter highlights the stories of remarkable individuals who have exemplified the Law of Responsibility, turning adversity into triumph.

1. Nelson Mandela: From Prisoner to President

Background:

Nelson Mandela, a South African anti-apartheid revolutionary, faced extraordinary adversity, including 27 years of imprisonment for his activism against the apartheid regime. Despite these hardships, Mandela took full responsibility for his life and his vision of a free and equal South Africa.

Transforming Challenges:

While in prison, Mandela engaged in deep self-reflection and used his time to study and strengthen his resolve. He understood that true leadership required a commitment to reconciliation and justice. Upon his release, Mandela continued his activism with a renewed focus on peaceful negotiation and unity.

Opportunities for Growth and Success:

Mandela's unwavering commitment to his principles and his ability to take responsibility for his actions led to the dismantling of apartheid. In 1994, he became South Africa's first black president, guiding the nation through a transformative period of reconciliation and nation-building. Mandela's legacy of forgiveness, leadership, and dedication to human rights continues to inspire the world.

2. J.K. Rowling: From Struggling Writer to Literary Icon

Background:

J.K. Rowling, the author of the Harry Potter series, faced significant personal and professional challenges before achieving literary success. As a single mother living on welfare, Rowling struggled with financial hardship and depression while pursuing her dream of becoming a writer.

Transforming Challenges:

Rowling took responsibility for her circumstances by committing to her writing. Despite numerous rejections from publishers, she persisted, driven by her belief in her story and her desire to create a better life for her daughter.

Opportunities for Growth and Success:

Rowling's perseverance paid off when Bloomsbury Publishing accepted her manuscript for publication. The Harry Potter series became a global phenomenon, selling over 500 million copies and being adapted into a successful film franchise. Rowling's journey from struggling writer to literary icon underscores the importance of resilience, self-belief, and continuous growth.

3. Oprah Winfrey: From Poverty to Media Mogul

Background:

Oprah Winfrey's journey from a challenging childhood to becoming one of the most influential women in the world is a testament to the power of personal growth and transformation. Born into poverty in rural Mississippi, Winfrey faced numerous hardships, including abuse and discrimination.

Transforming Challenges:

Despite her difficult upbringing, Winfrey's determination to succeed never wavered. She embraced education as a path to a better life and pursued a career in media with relentless drive. Winfrey took responsibility for her life by continuously seeking opportunities for personal and professional growth.

Opportunities for Growth and Success:

Winfrey's talk show, "The Oprah Winfrey Show," became the highest-rated television talk show in history, running for 25 years. She founded Harpo Productions, launched her own television network (OWN), and became a prominent philanthropist. Winfrey's commitment to personal growth, education, and empowerment has inspired millions worldwide, showcasing the transformative power of taking responsibility for one's life.

4. Richard Branson: Entrepreneurial Spirit and Resilience

Background:

Richard Branson, the founder of the Virgin Group, faced numerous challenges in his entrepreneurial journey. Despite struggling with dyslexia and leaving school at a young age, Branson pursued his passion for business with unrelenting enthusiasm.

Transforming Challenges:

Branson took responsibility for his learning difficulties and turned them into an advantage by developing creative solutions and a strong work ethic. He embraced failures as learning opportunities and persisted in his entrepreneurial endeavors despite setbacks.

Opportunities for Growth and Success:

Branson's innovative approach and resilience led to the creation of the Virgin Group, a multinational conglomerate with over 400 companies in various industries, including music, aviation, and space travel. His willingness to take risks and learn from his experiences has made him one of the most successful and adventurous entrepreneurs in the world.

5. Malala Yousafzai: Advocate for Girls' Education

Background:

Malala Yousafzai, a Pakistani education activist, faced life-threatening adversity in her fight for girls' education. At the age of 15, she survived an assassination attempt by the Taliban, who opposed her advocacy for education.

Transforming Challenges:

Despite the attack, Malala took responsibility for her cause and continued her activism on a global scale. She used her experiences to raise awareness about the importance of education for girls and to speak out against oppression and violence.

Opportunities for Growth and Success:

Malala's efforts have been recognized worldwide. In 2014, she became the youngest recipient of the Nobel Peace Prize. She founded the Malala Fund, which supports education initiatives for girls in various countries. Malala's resilience and dedication to her cause exemplify the power of taking responsibility for one's life and using adversity as a catalyst for change.

These real-life examples illustrate the transformative power of taking responsibility for one's life. By recognizing and accepting their power to shape their destinies, individuals like Nelson Mandela, J.K. Rowling, Oprah Winfrey, Richard

Branson, and Malala Yousafzai have turned significant challenges into opportunities for growth and success. Their stories inspire us to embrace the Law of Responsibility, overcome adversity with resilience and determination, and actively pursue our goals and aspirations. As we continue exploring the Law of Responsibility, let these examples guide and motivate us on our journey toward a more empowered, intentional, and fulfilling life.

CHAPTER 05

<hr>

THE LAW OF CONNECTION

The Interconnectedness of Life

The Law of Connection highlights the inherent interconnectedness of all life, emphasizing that our actions, thoughts, and relationships impact not only ourselves but also those around us and the broader world. This principle underscores the importance of understanding our place within the web of life and cultivating relationships, community, and empathy. This chapter explores the spiritual and practical implications of the Law of Connection, offering insights into how we can foster deeper connections and live more harmoniously with others.

Understanding the Law of Connection

The Law of Connection posits that everything in the universe is interlinked. Our actions, thoughts, and emotions create ripples that affect the lives of others and the environment. Recognizing this interconnectedness encourages us to act with greater awareness and responsibility, understanding that our choices have far-reaching consequences.

Key Aspects of the Law of Connection:

1. Interdependence: All living beings are interconnected and rely on each other for survival and well-being.

2. Empathy: Understanding and sharing the feelings of others is crucial for building strong relationships and communities.

3. Community: Human beings thrive in supportive and nurturing communities that foster collaboration and mutual respect.

4. Responsibility: Our actions impact others, and we have a responsibility to consider the broader effects of our behavior.

The Spiritual Implications of Interconnectedness

On a spiritual level, the Law of Connection teaches us that we are part of a greater whole. This understanding fosters a sense of unity and compassion, as we recognize that our well-being is intertwined with the well-being of others.

1. Unity: Spiritual traditions around the world emphasize the concept of oneness, teaching that we are all connected by a universal spirit or life force.

2. Compassion: Recognizing our interconnectedness inspires compassion and empathy, encouraging us to act with kindness and consideration for others.

3. Purpose: Understanding our place within the web of life can give us a sense of purpose and meaning, motivating us to contribute positively to the world.

Practical Implications of Interconnectedness

In practical terms, the Law of Connection influences how we interact with others and the environment. By fostering positive relationships and acting with empathy and responsibility, we can create a more harmonious and sustainable world.

1. Building Relationships:

- Strong, positive relationships are the foundation of a connected life. Invest time and effort in nurturing your relationships with family, friends, colleagues, and neighbors.

- Practice active listening, open communication, and empathy to deepen your connections with others.

2. Fostering Community:

- Engage in community activities and support local initiatives that promote collaboration and mutual respect.

- Volunteer your time and skills to help others and contribute to the well-being of your community.

3. Practicing Empathy:

- Cultivate empathy by putting yourself in others' shoes and understanding their perspectives and emotions.

- Practice kindness and compassion in your daily interactions, recognizing the impact of your actions on others.

4. Environmental Responsibility:

- Acknowledge the interconnectedness of all life by adopting sustainable practices that protect the environment.

- Reduce your ecological footprint by conserving resources, reducing waste, and supporting eco-friendly initiatives.

Strategies for Embracing the Law of Connection

To fully embrace the Law of Connection, consider the following strategies:

1. Develop Self-Awareness:

- Reflect on your actions, thoughts, and emotions, and consider how they impact others and the environment.

- Practice mindfulness and meditation to enhance your self-awareness and connection to the present moment.

2. Practice Gratitude:

- Cultivate an attitude of gratitude by acknowledging the positive aspects of your life and the contributions of others.

- Express your gratitude to those around you, strengthening your relationships and fostering a sense of community.

3. Engage in Service:

- Volunteer for causes that resonate with you and contribute to the greater good.

- Engage in acts of kindness and service, recognizing that helping others enhances your own well-being.

4. Foster Inclusive Environments:

- Create inclusive spaces that celebrate diversity and promote mutual respect and understanding.

- Advocate for social justice and equality, recognizing the interconnectedness of all individuals and communities.

5. Support Collaborative Efforts:

- Encourage collaboration and teamwork in your personal and professional life.

- Participate in group activities and projects that promote shared goals and collective well-being.

Real-Life Examples of Interconnectedness

1. Jane Goodall: Advocate for Wildlife and Communities

- Jane Goodall, a renowned primatologist, has dedicated her life to studying chimpanzees and advocating for wildlife conservation. Her work highlights the interconnectedness of humans and animals, emphasizing the importance of preserving natural habitats for the well-being of all species.

- Goodall's efforts have not only advanced scientific understanding but also fostered global awareness and action to protect endangered species and their ecosystems.

2. Wangari Maathai: Environmental and Social Activist

- Wangari Maathai, founder of the Green Belt Movement in Kenya, recognized the interconnectedness of environmental sustainability and community development. Her organization focuses on tree planting, environmental conservation, and women's empowerment.

- Maathai's work has led to the planting of millions of trees, the restoration of degraded landscapes, and the improvement of livelihoods for countless communities. Her legacy demonstrates the power of interconnected action to create positive change.

3. Fred Rogers: Cultivating Kindness and Empathy

- Fred Rogers, the beloved host of "Mister Rogers' Neighborhood," dedicated his career to promoting kindness, empathy, and understanding among children and adults. Through his television show, Rogers taught valuable lessons about the importance of relationships, community, and emotional well-being.

- Rogers' compassionate approach and emphasis on connection continue to inspire generations, highlighting the lasting impact of empathy and kindness.

Practical Exercises for Embracing Interconnectedness

1. Mindful Observation:

- Spend time in nature and observe the interconnectedness of the natural world. Reflect on how different elements—plants, animals, water, and air—interact and support each other.

- Use this time to appreciate the beauty and complexity of life and consider how your actions influence the environment.

2. Empathy Journaling:

- Keep a journal to record your reflections on empathy and connection. Write about your interactions with others, focusing on moments of empathy, kindness, and understanding.

- Reflect on how these experiences enhance your sense of connection and well-being.

3. Community Involvement:

- Get involved in community activities, such as local events, volunteer opportunities, or neighborhood groups. Engage with others and contribute to initiatives that promote collaboration and mutual support.

- Reflect on how your involvement strengthens your sense of community and interconnectedness.

4. Gratitude Practice:

- Practice gratitude by writing down three things you are grateful for each day. Consider the people, experiences, and elements of nature that contribute to your well-being.

- Express your gratitude to those around you, strengthening your relationships and fostering a positive atmosphere.

5. Collaborative Projects:

- Participate in collaborative projects at work, school, or in your community. Focus on teamwork, communication, and shared goals.

- Reflect on how working together enhances your sense of connection and achieves greater outcomes than individual efforts.

The Law of Connection emphasizes the inherent interconnectedness of all life, reminding us that our actions, thoughts, and relationships impact the broader world. By understanding and embracing this interconnectedness, we can cultivate empathy, build strong relationships, and contribute to our communities. Strategies such as developing self-awareness, practicing gratitude, engaging in service, fostering inclusive environments, and supporting collaborative efforts help us live more harmoniously with others. Real-life examples of individuals like Jane Goodall, Wangari Maathai, and Fred Rogers inspire us to recognize and honor the connections that bind us all. As we continue exploring the Law of Connection, let these insights guide us toward a more compassionate, responsible, and fulfilling life, where we actively contribute to the well-being of all living beings.

Building Relationships

Effective Communication: Techniques for Fostering Open and Honest Communication

Effective communication is the foundation of building strong, healthy relationships. It involves not just the exchange of information, but also understanding the emotions and intentions behind the information. Effective communication fosters trust, resolves conflicts, and creates a sense of connection and understanding. This chapter explores the importance of effective communication, its benefits, and practical techniques for fostering open and honest communication in all aspects of life.

The Importance of Effective Communication

Effective communication is essential for several reasons:

1. Building Trust: Open and honest communication is key to establishing and maintaining trust in relationships.

2. Conflict Resolution: Clear and respectful communication helps resolve conflicts and misunderstandings.

3. Emotional Connection: Sharing thoughts and feelings fosters emotional intimacy and strengthens bonds.

4. Collaboration: Effective communication enhances teamwork and collaboration in personal and professional settings.

5. Personal Growth: Communicating effectively improves self-awareness and personal development.

Key Principles of Effective Communication

1. Clarity: Communicate your thoughts and ideas clearly and concisely.

2. Active Listening: Pay full attention to the speaker, show empathy, and provide feedback.

3. Nonverbal Communication: Be aware of body language, facial expressions, and tone of voice.

4. Respect: Communicate with respect and consideration for the other person's perspective.

5. Feedback: Provide and seek constructive feedback to improve understanding and performance.

Techniques for Fostering Open and Honest Communication

To enhance your communication skills and foster open and honest communication, consider the following techniques:

1. Practice Active Listening:

- Focus fully on the speaker without interrupting. Show that you are listening through nodding, maintaining eye contact, and using verbal acknowledgments like "I see" or "I understand."

- Reflect back what the speaker has said to confirm understanding. For example, "So what you're saying is..."

2. Use "I" Statements:

- Express your feelings and thoughts using "I" statements to take ownership of your emotions and reduce defensiveness. For example, "I feel upset when..." instead of "You make me upset when..."

- This approach helps to communicate personal experiences without blaming others.

3. Be Clear and Concise:

- Articulate your thoughts clearly and avoid using ambiguous language. Stick to the main points and avoid unnecessary details.

- Ensure your message is straightforward and easily understood.

4. Pay Attention to Nonverbal Cues:

- Be aware of your body language, facial expressions, and tone of voice. Ensure that your nonverbal cues align with your verbal message.

- Observe the other person's nonverbal cues to gain insight into their feelings and reactions.

5. Practice Empathy:

- Try to understand the other person's perspective and feelings. Show empathy by acknowledging their emotions and validating their experiences.

- Use phrases like "I can see how that would be frustrating" or "It sounds like you're feeling..."

6. Create a Safe Environment:

- Foster an environment where everyone feels comfortable expressing their thoughts and feelings without fear of judgment or retaliation.

- Encourage open dialogue by being approachable, patient, and nonjudgmental.

7. Ask Open-Ended Questions:

- Use open-ended questions to encourage deeper conversation and understanding. These questions require more than a yes or no answer and prompt the speaker to elaborate.

- Examples include "Can you tell me more about that?" or "How did that make you feel?"

8. Manage Emotions:

- Stay calm and composed during conversations, especially during conflicts. Take deep breaths or pause if you feel overwhelmed.

- Address your emotions before engaging in difficult conversations to ensure you communicate effectively and respectfully.

9. Provide Constructive Feedback:

- Offer feedback that is specific, actionable, and focused on behaviors rather than personal characteristics. Use the "sandwich" method by starting with a positive comment, followed by constructive feedback, and ending with another positive comment.

- Encourage feedback from others to improve your communication and interpersonal skills.

10. Be Open and Honest:

- Communicate openly and honestly, sharing your thoughts and feelings authentically. Avoid hiding important information or being evasive.

- Transparency builds trust and fosters deeper connections.

Practical Exercises for Improving Communication

1. Active Listening Practice:

- Pair up with a partner and take turns speaking and listening. Practice active listening by summarizing what the speaker has said and asking clarifying questions.

- Reflect on the experience and discuss what worked well and what could be improved.

2. Role-Playing Scenarios:

- Role-play different communication scenarios, such as resolving a conflict, giving feedback, or expressing emotions. Practice using "I" statements, active listening, and empathy.

- Discuss the outcomes and identify areas for improvement.

3. Nonverbal Communication Awareness:

- Record yourself during a conversation and review the recording to observe your nonverbal communication. Pay attention to your body language, facial expressions, and tone of voice.

- Make adjustments to ensure your nonverbal cues align with your verbal messages.

4. Empathy Exercises:

- Engage in exercises that promote empathy, such as reading books or watching movies that depict different perspectives and experiences. Reflect on how these stories made you feel and how you can apply empathy in your interactions.

- Practice empathy in your daily interactions by actively listening and validating others' emotions.

5. Feedback Exchange:

- Pair up with a partner and exchange feedback on specific behaviors or interactions. Use the "sandwich" method to provide constructive feedback and discuss how it was received.

- Use the feedback to make improvements and enhance your communication skills.

Real-Life Examples of Effective Communication

1. Barack Obama: Inspiring Leadership through Communication

- Barack Obama, the 44th President of the United States, is renowned for his effective communication skills. His ability to articulate his vision clearly, connect with diverse audiences, and inspire change through powerful speeches and empathetic interactions exemplifies the impact of effective communication.

- Obama's use of storytelling, empathy, and active listening helped build trust and fostered a sense of unity and purpose.

2. Brené Brown: Promoting Vulnerability and Empathy

- Brené Brown, a research professor and author, emphasizes the importance of vulnerability and empathy in communication. Her work highlights how sharing our true selves and listening with empathy can strengthen relationships and build trust.

- Brown's TED Talk on vulnerability has resonated with millions, demonstrating how open and honest communication fosters connection and understanding.

3. Nelson Mandela: Reconciliation through Dialogue

- Nelson Mandela's approach to reconciliation in post-apartheid South Africa underscores the power of effective communication. Mandela used open dialogue, active listening, and empathy to bridge divides and foster national unity.

- His emphasis on forgiveness and understanding helped heal a fractured nation and demonstrated the transformative potential of communication.

Effective communication is the foundation of building strong, healthy relationships. By practicing active listening, using "I" statements, being clear and concise, and fostering empathy, we can enhance our communication skills and foster open and honest interactions. Real-life examples of effective communicators, like Barack Obama, Brené Brown, and Nelson Mandela, inspire us to prioritize communication in our relationships and communities. As we continue exploring the Law of Connection, let these techniques guide us toward more meaningful and impactful interactions, where trust, understanding, and collaboration flourish.

Empathy and Compassion: Cultivating Empathy and Compassion in Daily Interactions

Empathy and compassion are essential components of effective communication and strong relationships. They involve understanding and sharing the feelings of others and responding with kindness and support. Cultivating empathy and compassion in our daily interactions can lead to deeper connections, reduced conflicts, and a more harmonious life. This chapter explores the importance of empathy and compassion, their benefits, and practical strategies for incorporating these qualities into everyday interactions.

Understanding Empathy and Compassion

Empathy is the ability to understand and share the feelings of another person. It involves putting yourself in someone else's shoes and experiencing their emotions from their perspective. There are three types of empathy:

1. Cognitive Empathy: Understanding someone's thoughts and perspectives.

2. Emotional Empathy: Sharing and feeling someone else's emotions.

3. Compassionate Empathy: Understanding and feeling someone's emotions and taking action to help.

Compassion goes a step further by not only understanding and sharing someone's feelings but also having a desire to alleviate their suffering and contribute to their well-being. It involves kindness, support, and a genuine concern for others.

The Importance of Empathy and Compassion

Empathy and compassion are crucial for several reasons:

1. Building Strong Relationships: These qualities foster trust, understanding, and emotional connection, which are essential for strong, healthy relationships.

2. Conflict Resolution: Empathy and compassion help de-escalate conflicts by promoting understanding and mutual respect.

3. Emotional Support: Providing empathy and compassion helps others feel heard, valued, and supported.

4. Promoting Well-Being: Acts of empathy and compassion contribute to the overall well-being of individuals and communities.

5. Personal Growth: Cultivating empathy and compassion enhances self-awareness and emotional intelligence.

Strategies for Cultivating Empathy and Compassion

To cultivate empathy and compassion in daily interactions, consider the following strategies:

1. Active Listening:

- Pay full attention to the speaker without interrupting. Show that you are listening through nodding, maintaining eye contact, and using verbal acknowledgments like "I see" or "I understand."

- Reflect back what the speaker has said to confirm understanding. For example, "So what you're saying is..."

2. Practice Perspective-Taking:

- Try to see situations from the other person's point of view. Ask yourself how you would feel and react if you were in their position.

- Use questions like "How would I feel if this happened to me?" or "What might they be experiencing right now?"

3. Show Emotional Support:

- Offer comfort and reassurance to those who are struggling. Simple acts like a kind word, a hug, or a listening ear can make a significant difference.

- Use empathetic statements like "I'm here for you" or "I can see that this is really tough for you."

4. Be Present:

- Fully engage with others during conversations and interactions. Avoid distractions and give them your undivided attention.

- Practice mindfulness to stay present and attentive in your interactions.

5. Express Kindness:

- Perform acts of kindness regularly, such as helping a neighbor, giving a compliment, or supporting a colleague.

- Show appreciation and gratitude to others, acknowledging their efforts and contributions.

6. Develop Self-Compassion:

- Treat yourself with the same kindness and understanding that you offer to others. Recognize your own needs and take steps to care for your well-being.

- Practice self-compassion by being gentle with yourself during times of struggle or failure.

7. Educate Yourself:

- Learn about different cultures, perspectives, and experiences to broaden your understanding and empathy.

- Read books, watch documentaries, and engage in conversations that challenge your assumptions and expand your worldview.

8. Engage in Reflective Practices:

- Reflect on your interactions and consider how you can improve your empathy and compassion. Use journaling or meditation to gain insights and enhance self-awareness.

- Set intentions for how you will incorporate empathy and compassion into your daily life.

Real-Life Examples of Empathy and Compassion

1. Mahatma Gandhi: Champion of Nonviolence and Empathy

- Mahatma Gandhi's philosophy of nonviolence (Ahimsa) and empathy towards all living beings guided his leadership in the Indian independence movement. He demonstrated deep compassion for the oppressed and used empathy to understand their struggles, advocating for peaceful resistance and justice.

- Gandhi's ability to connect with people from all walks of life and his commitment to compassion and nonviolence left a lasting legacy of empathy-driven leadership.

2. Mother Teresa: A Life of Compassionate Service

- Mother Teresa dedicated her life to serving the poorest and most vulnerable individuals. Her empathy and compassion drove her to provide care, love, and support to those in need, often at great personal sacrifice.

- Through her work with the Missionaries of Charity, Mother Teresa exemplified the transformative power of compassion in alleviating suffering and fostering human dignity.

3. Fred Rogers: Promoting Kindness and Understanding

- Fred Rogers, the beloved host of "Mister Rogers' Neighborhood," promoted empathy, kindness, and understanding through his television show. He taught children the importance of expressing their feelings, understanding others, and showing compassion.

- Rogers' gentle and empathetic approach helped children and adults alike feel valued and understood, creating a lasting impact on generations.

Practical Exercises for Cultivating Empathy and Compassion

1. Empathy Journaling:

- Keep a journal to record your reflections on empathy and compassion. Write about your interactions with others, focusing on moments of empathy, kindness, and understanding.

- Reflect on how these experiences enhance your sense of connection and well-being.

2. Random Acts of Kindness:

- Perform random acts of kindness each day. These can be small gestures, like holding the door for someone, paying for a stranger's coffee, or sending a thank-you note.

- Reflect on how these acts make you feel and how they impact others.

3. Mindfulness Meditation:

- Practice mindfulness meditation to cultivate presence and awareness. Focus on your breath and observe your thoughts and feelings without judgment.

- Use loving-kindness meditation to send positive intentions to yourself and others, enhancing your capacity for empathy and compassion.

4. Empathy Mapping:

- Create an empathy map to better understand someone's perspective. Divide a paper into four sections: Thinking, Feeling, Seeing, and Doing. Fill in each section with what you think the person might be experiencing in these areas.

- Use the empathy map to gain insights into their perspective and consider how you can respond with empathy and compassion.

5. Volunteer and Serve:

- Engage in volunteer work or community service that allows you to connect with and support others. Choose causes that resonate with you and where you can make a meaningful impact.

- Reflect on your experiences and how they enhance your understanding of empathy and compassion.

Empathy and compassion are essential qualities for fostering strong, healthy relationships and creating a more harmonious world. By practicing active listening, perspective-taking, showing emotional support, and engaging in acts of kindness, we can cultivate empathy and compassion in our daily interactions. Real-life examples of individuals like Mahatma Gandhi, Mother Teresa, and Fred Rogers inspire us to prioritize these qualities in our lives. As we continue exploring the Law of Connection, let these strategies guide us toward more meaningful and impactful interactions, where empathy and compassion become the foundation of our relationships and communities.

Community Building: Strategies for Creating and Nurturing Supportive Communities

Community building is essential for fostering a sense of belonging, support, and mutual growth. A strong community provides a network of individuals who share common values, goals, and interests, and who support one another through life's challenges and triumphs. This chapter explores the importance of community building, the benefits of being part of a supportive community, and practical strategies for creating and nurturing such communities.

The Importance of Community Building

1. Sense of Belonging: Communities provide a sense of belonging and identity, helping individuals feel connected and valued.

2. Support and Resources: Communities offer emotional, social, and practical support, enhancing members' resilience and well-being.

3. Shared Goals and Values: Communities bring people together around common goals and values, fostering collaboration and collective action.

4. Personal Growth: Being part of a community encourages personal growth through shared learning, experiences, and opportunities.

5. Enhanced Well-Being: Social connections and a sense of community contribute to overall happiness and mental health.

Strategies for Creating and Nurturing Supportive Communities

1. Identify Common Interests and Goals:

- Gather people who share similar interests, values, or goals. This common ground provides a strong foundation for building a cohesive community.

- Identify the purpose and objectives of the community, whether it's for social support, professional networking, or a shared hobby or cause.

2. Foster Open and Inclusive Communication:

- Create an environment where all members feel comfortable expressing their thoughts and ideas. Encourage open, honest, and respectful communication.

- Use various communication channels, such as meetings, social media, and group chats, to keep everyone informed and engaged.

3. Organize Regular Gatherings and Activities:

- Plan regular events, meetings, or activities that bring community members together. These can include social gatherings, workshops, volunteer projects, or discussion groups.

- Ensure that activities are inclusive and cater to the diverse interests and needs of the community.

4. Encourage Participation and Collaboration:

- Involve community members in decision-making processes and encourage them to take on active roles and responsibilities.

- Foster a collaborative culture where members work together on projects, share resources, and support each other's initiatives.

5. Provide Support and Resources:

- Offer resources and support to community members, such as educational materials, access to services, or networking opportunities.

- Create a system for members to request and offer help, ensuring that everyone feels supported.

6. Celebrate Achievements and Milestones:

- Recognize and celebrate the achievements and milestones of community members and the community as a whole. This fosters a sense of pride and motivation.

- Hold appreciation events or share success stories to highlight the positive impact of the community.

7. Build a Positive and Inclusive Culture:

- Promote values such as respect, kindness, and inclusivity within the community. Address conflicts and issues promptly and constructively.

- Create guidelines or a code of conduct to ensure that all members uphold the community's values and standards.

8. Leverage Technology:

- Utilize digital tools and platforms to facilitate communication, collaboration, and information sharing. Online communities can complement in-person interactions and expand reach.

- Use social media, forums, and collaboration tools to keep members connected and engaged.

9. Provide Opportunities for Personal and Collective Growth:

- Offer opportunities for learning and development, such as workshops, training sessions, or mentoring programs.

- Encourage members to share their skills and knowledge, fostering a culture of continuous growth and mutual support.

10. Evaluate and Adapt:

- Regularly assess the community's activities, goals, and member satisfaction. Seek feedback and make adjustments to improve the community's effectiveness and relevance.

- Stay flexible and open to change, adapting to the evolving needs and interests of the community.

Real-Life Examples of Successful Community Building

1. Toastmasters International:

- Toastmasters International is a global organization that helps individuals improve their public speaking and leadership skills. Local clubs provide a supportive community where members practice and develop their skills through regular meetings and activities.

- The organization fosters a positive and collaborative environment, encouraging members to support and learn from each other.

2. Habitat for Humanity:

- Habitat for Humanity is a nonprofit organization that builds affordable housing for families in need. The organization brings together volunteers, donors, and community members to work on construction projects.

- By involving the community in its mission, Habitat for Humanity fosters a sense of shared purpose and collective action.

3. Mothers Against Drunk Driving (MADD):

- MADD is an organization dedicated to preventing drunk driving and supporting victims of drunk driving accidents. It provides a platform for individuals affected by drunk driving to connect, share their stories, and advocate for change.

- MADD's community-building efforts have created a strong network of support and advocacy, driving legislative changes and raising awareness.

Practical Exercises for Community Building

1. Community Mapping:

- Identify the strengths, resources, and needs of your community. Create a map that highlights key members, organizations, and assets.

- Use this map to identify opportunities for collaboration and resource sharing.

2. Listening Circles:

- Organize listening circles where community members can share their experiences, ideas, and concerns in a safe and supportive environment.

- Use active listening techniques to ensure that everyone feels heard and valued.

3. Skill Sharing Workshops:

- Host workshops where community members can share their skills and knowledge with others. Encourage members to lead sessions on topics they are passionate about.

- Promote a culture of continuous learning and mutual support.

4. Volunteer Projects:

- Plan and execute volunteer projects that address community needs and bring members together. This can include activities such as neighborhood cleanups, fundraising events, or support for local nonprofits.

- Reflect on the impact of these projects and celebrate the contributions of community members.

5. Mentorship Programs:

- Establish mentorship programs that pair experienced members with those seeking guidance and support. Encourage regular check-ins and goal setting.

- Use mentorship to foster personal and professional growth within the community.

Community building is essential for creating a sense of belonging, support, and mutual growth. By fostering open communication, organizing regular activities, encouraging participation, and providing support and resources, we can create and nurture supportive communities. Real-life examples of successful community building, such as Toastmasters International, Habitat for Humanity, and Mothers Against Drunk Driving, demonstrate the power of collective action and shared purpose. As we continue exploring the Law of Connection, let these strategies guide us toward building strong, supportive communities that enhance our lives and contribute to the greater good.

CHAPTER 06

REAL-LIFE EXAMPLES

Stories of Individuals and Communities Harnessing the Power of Connection

The Law of Connection emphasizes the profound impact that strong relationships and a sense of community can have on our lives. By harnessing the power of connection, individuals and communities can create positive change, foster resilience, and build a better future. This chapter presents inspiring stories of people and groups who have leveraged their connections to make a significant impact, illustrating the transformative potential of this law.

1. Malala Yousafzai: Global Advocate for Education

Background:

Malala Yousafzai, a Pakistani activist for female education, became a global symbol of courage and resilience after surviving an assassination attempt by the Taliban. Despite the threats and violence she faced, Malala continued to advocate for girls' education, using her voice to inspire change.

Harnessing the Power of Connection:

Malala's story is a testament to the power of connection. She connected with people worldwide through her advocacy, drawing attention to the plight of girls denied education. Malala co-founded the Malala Fund, which connects activists, educators, and policymakers to support education initiatives globally.

Impact:

Through her connections, Malala has influenced global education policies and provided funding for educational projects in countries where girls' education is under threat. Her work has empowered countless young women to pursue their dreams and break barriers, demonstrating the transformative power of connection.

2. Jane Goodall: Champion for Wildlife Conservation

Background:

Jane Goodall, a renowned primatologist and anthropologist, has dedicated her life to studying chimpanzees and advocating for wildlife conservation. Her groundbreaking research in Tanzania transformed our understanding of primates and highlighted the urgent need for conservation efforts.

Harnessing the Power of Connection:

Goodall's work connects people to the natural world, fostering a sense of responsibility and stewardship for the environment. She founded the Jane Goodall Institute, which connects scientists, conservationists, and communities to protect wildlife habitats and promote sustainable development.

Impact:

Goodall's efforts have led to significant advancements in wildlife conservation and environmental education. Through her Roots & Shoots program, she has connected young people worldwide, empowering them to take action in their communities to create positive environmental change.

3. Bryan Stevenson: Advocate for Justice and Equality

Background:

Bryan Stevenson, a lawyer and social justice activist, founded the Equal Justice Initiative (EJI) to provide legal representation to marginalized and disadvantaged individuals.

Stevenson's work addresses systemic injustices in the criminal justice system and advocates for racial equality.

Harnessing the Power of Connection:

Stevenson has built a network of lawyers, activists, and community leaders to address issues of mass incarceration, racial injustice, and the death penalty. Through EJI, he connects individuals and communities to legal resources, education, and advocacy tools.

Impact:

Stevenson's efforts have resulted in numerous legal victories, including the release of wrongly convicted individuals and significant reforms in the criminal justice system. His work has raised awareness about racial inequality and inspired a broader movement for justice and human rights.

4. Wangari Maathai: Environmental and Social Activist

Background:

Wangari Maathai, a Kenyan environmentalist and political activist, founded the Green Belt Movement to address deforestation and environmental degradation in Kenya. Her work focused on tree planting, environmental conservation, and women's empowerment.

Harnessing the Power of Connection:

Maathai connected local communities, particularly women, to environmental conservation efforts. She mobilized people to plant trees, restore degraded lands, and advocate for sustainable practices. Her work linked environmental health with social and economic development.

Impact:

The Green Belt Movement has planted millions of trees, revitalizing ecosystems and improving the livelihoods of communities. Maathai's work earned her the Nobel Peace Prize and inspired global environmental movements, demonstrating the power of grassroots connections to drive change.

5. Fred Rogers: Cultivating Kindness and Empathy

Background:

Fred Rogers, the beloved host of "Mister Rogers' Neighborhood," dedicated his career to promoting kindness, empathy, and understanding among children and adults. His gentle, compassionate approach touched the lives of millions, fostering a culture of care and respect.

Harnessing the Power of Connection:

Rogers used television to connect with his audience personally, addressing complex emotions and social issues in a relatable and accessible way. His emphasis on emotional intelligence and empathy helped viewers feel understood and valued.

Impact:

Rogers' legacy continues to influence generations through his timeless messages of kindness and empathy. His work has inspired educators, parents, and mental health professionals to prioritize emotional well-being and compassionate communication.

Practical Exercises for Harnessing the Power of Connection

1. Community Engagement:

- Identify local organizations or initiatives that align with your values and interests. Volunteer your time, skills, or resources to support their efforts.

- Build connections with community members by attending events, joining discussion groups, or participating in collaborative projects.

2. Network Building:

- Create a network of individuals who share your goals and values. Reach out to potential collaborators, mentors, or partners to build mutually beneficial relationships.

- Organize regular meetups, virtual gatherings, or workshops to strengthen your network and foster collaboration.

3. Advocacy and Awareness:

- Use your voice and platform to raise awareness about issues that matter to you. Share information, stories, and resources to educate and inspire others.

- Connect with advocacy groups or movements that align with your cause, and participate in campaigns, petitions, or public events.

4. Empathy and Compassion Practice:

- Practice empathy and compassion in your daily interactions by actively listening, showing kindness, and offering support to others.

- Engage in reflective practices, such as journaling or meditation, to enhance your understanding of others' perspectives and experiences.

5. Collaboration and Teamwork:

- Foster a collaborative culture in your personal and professional life. Encourage teamwork, open communication, and mutual respect in group projects and activities.

- Celebrate collective achievements and recognize the contributions of each member.

The stories of Malala Yousafzai, Jane Goodall, Bryan Stevenson, Wangari Maathai, and Fred Rogers illustrate the profound impact of harnessing the power of connection. By building strong relationships, fostering empathy, and mobilizing communities, these individuals have created positive change and inspired others to do the same. Their examples demonstrate that the Law of Connection can drive transformative action and foster a more just, compassionate, and sustainable world. As we continue exploring the Law of Connection, let these stories inspire us to leverage our connections to create meaningful impact and build a better future for all.

INTERGRATINGTHE LAWS

Integrating the Laws: A Roadmap for a Life of Purpose, Fulfillment, and Joy

As we conclude our exploration of the five laws of life, it's essential to understand how these principles interconnect and reinforce one another. By integrating these laws into our daily lives, we can create a life filled with purpose, fulfillment, and joy. This final chapter summarizes the five laws and provides practical advice for applying them in a cohesive and harmonious way.

The Five Laws of Life

1. The Law of Attraction: This law states that our thoughts and feelings attract corresponding experiences and outcomes. By focusing on positive thinking, visualization, and emotional alignment, we can manifest our deepest desires.

2. The Law of Cause and Effect: Also known as karma, this law dictates that every action has a corresponding reaction. Understanding this law emphasizes the importance of conscious actions and decisions, recognizing that we are responsible for the consequences of our behavior.

3. The Law of Growth: Growth is a fundamental aspect of life, necessitating constant learning and adaptation. This law encourages us to embrace change, strive for self-improvement, and view challenges as opportunities for growth.

4. The Law of Responsibility: This law asserts that we are the architects of our own lives. It emphasizes taking ownership of our actions, decisions, and circumstances, empowering us to create the life we desire.

5. The Law of Connection: Highlighting the inherent interconnectedness of all life, this law underscores the importance of relationships, community, and empathy. Recognizing our interconnectedness fosters compassion and collective well-being.

Practical Advice for Integrating the Laws

1. Cultivate Positive Thinking and Visualization:

- Practice daily affirmations to reinforce positive beliefs and visualize your goals with clarity and emotion.

- Surround yourself with positive influences and environments that support your aspirations.

2. Take Conscious Actions:

- Be mindful of the impact of your actions and decisions on yourself and others. Strive to act with integrity and kindness.

- Reflect on past actions to learn from them and make better choices moving forward.

3. Embrace Continuous Learning and Growth:

- Set personal and professional development goals and pursue new knowledge and skills regularly.

- View challenges and setbacks as opportunities for growth and learning, and remain adaptable to change.

4. Take Ownership of Your Life:

- Accept responsibility for your actions and their outcomes. Avoid blaming external factors and focus on what you can control.

- Develop a proactive mindset by setting clear goals, creating action plans, and taking consistent steps toward your objectives.

5. Foster Strong Relationships and Community:

- Invest time and effort in building and nurturing meaningful relationships. Practice empathy, active listening, and open communication.

- Engage in community activities, support local initiatives, and contribute to collective well-being.

Integrating the Laws into Daily Living

1. Morning Routine:

- Begin your day with a morning routine that incorporates meditation, positive affirmations, and visualization exercises. This sets a positive tone for the day and aligns your mindset with your goals.

2. Mindfulness Practice:

- Practice mindfulness throughout the day to stay present and aware of your thoughts, emotions, and actions. Use mindfulness techniques to manage stress and maintain focus.

3. Reflection and Journaling:

- Set aside time each day for reflection and journaling. Use this time to review your actions, celebrate your successes, and identify areas for improvement. Reflect on how the five laws are influencing your life.

4. Goal Setting and Action Planning:

- Regularly set and review your goals, breaking them down into actionable steps. Create detailed action plans and track your progress, adjusting as needed.

5. Community Involvement:

- Participate in community events, volunteer work, or social groups that align with your values and interests. Build connections and contribute to the collective well-being.

6. Gratitude Practice:

- Cultivate an attitude of gratitude by acknowledging and appreciating the positive aspects of your life. Express gratitude to others and recognize their contributions to your well-being.

The five laws of life—Attraction, Cause and Effect, Growth, Responsibility, and Connection—are powerful principles that can transform our lives when integrated harmoniously. By cultivating positive thinking, taking conscious actions, embracing continuous learning, owning our lives, and fostering strong relationships, we can create a life filled with purpose, fulfillment, and joy. These laws are interconnected, each reinforcing and enhancing the others, providing a comprehensive roadmap for living a meaningful and impactful life.

As you move forward, remember that the journey of integrating these laws is ongoing. Embrace the process with patience, persistence, and an open heart. Let these principles guide you toward a life of intentionality, growth, and connection, where you not only achieve your personal aspirations but also contribute positively to the world around you. By living in alignment with these laws, you can unlock your full potential and experience the profound joy that comes from living a life of purpose and fulfillment.

Moving Forward

Embracing the Journey of Self-Discovery and Growth

As we conclude our exploration of the five laws of life, it's important to remember that the journey of self-discovery and growth is continuous. Each day presents new opportunities to learn, adapt, and evolve. Encouraging a mindset of curiosity and resilience will empower you to navigate life's challenges and seize its possibilities. This final section highlights the importance of continuous learning and adaptation, offering guidance for maintaining momentum on your path to personal and professional fulfillment.

The Importance of Continuous Learning and Adaptation

1. Lifelong Learning: Embrace the idea that learning is a lifelong process. Whether through formal education, personal experiences, or interactions with others, there are always new skills to acquire and knowledge to gain.

2. Adaptability: The ability to adapt to changing circumstances is crucial for growth. Life is dynamic, and being

flexible allows you to respond effectively to new challenges and opportunities.

3. Curiosity: Maintain a curious mindset. Ask questions, seek new experiences, and explore different perspectives. Curiosity fuels innovation and personal development.

4. Resilience: Build resilience by viewing setbacks as learning opportunities. Develop coping strategies to manage stress and maintain a positive outlook in the face of adversity.

Practical Strategies for Continuous Learning and Growth

1. Set Learning Goals:

- Regularly set and review learning goals that align with your personal and professional aspirations. These could include acquiring new skills, expanding your knowledge in a particular field, or exploring new hobbies.

2. Engage in Reflective Practices:

- Make time for regular self-reflection through journaling, meditation, or quiet contemplation. Reflect on your experiences, identify lessons learned, and set intentions for the future.

3. Seek Feedback:

- Actively seek feedback from others to gain different perspectives on your actions and decisions. Use this feedback to make informed adjustments and improve your performance.

4. Embrace Challenges:

- View challenges as opportunities for growth. Step out of your comfort zone and take on tasks that stretch your abilities. Embracing challenges builds confidence and competence.

5. Cultivate a Growth Mindset:

- Adopt a growth mindset by believing that your abilities and intelligence can be developed through effort and perseverance. Focus on learning and improvement rather than fearing failure.

6. Stay Curious and Open-Minded:

- Cultivate curiosity by exploring new interests, asking questions, and seeking out diverse experiences. Stay open to new ideas and perspectives, even if they challenge your current beliefs.

7. Invest in Relationships:

- Build and nurture relationships with people who inspire and support your growth. Engage in meaningful conversations, collaborate on projects, and learn from each other's experiences.

8. Participate in Continuous Education:

- Take advantage of educational opportunities, such as workshops, courses, seminars, and conferences. Stay updated with trends and advancements in your field.

Real-Life Applications of Continuous Learning and Adaptation

1. Personal Growth:

- Continuously seek self-improvement by setting personal development goals. This could involve improving your emotional intelligence, learning a new language, or developing a new hobby.

- Embrace a healthy lifestyle by staying physically active, maintaining a balanced diet, and practicing mindfulness to support your overall well-being.

2. Professional Development:

- Stay competitive in your career by acquiring new skills and knowledge relevant to your industry. Seek certifications, attend training programs, and participate in professional networks.

- Adapt to changes in the workplace by being flexible and proactive. Embrace new technologies, methodologies, and work environments.

3. Community Involvement:

- Engage with your community by participating in local initiatives, volunteering, and supporting social causes.

Building strong community connections enhances your sense of belonging and purpose.

- Lead or join community groups focused on learning and growth, such as book clubs, discussion groups, or skill-sharing workshops.

Encouragement for the Journey Ahead

As you move forward on your journey of self-discovery and growth, remember that progress often comes in small, incremental steps. Celebrate your achievements, no matter how minor they may seem, and stay motivated by acknowledging your growth over time. Surround yourself with supportive individuals who encourage your development and share your commitment to continuous learning.

Stay resilient in the face of challenges, understanding that setbacks are a natural part of the growth process. Use these experiences to build strength and adaptability, and keep your curiosity alive by exploring new ideas and experiences. By integrating the principles of the five laws of life into your daily practices, you can create a fulfilling and impactful life.

Embrace the journey with an open heart and mind, knowing that each step forward brings you closer to your highest potential. The path of continuous learning and growth is endless, and it is in this journey that you will find true fulfillment and joy. Keep striving, keep learning, and keep growing, for the possibilities are limitless.

Your life is your greatest masterpiece—craft it with intention, passion, and the wisdom of the five laws of life.

APPENDICES

APENDIX A, B, C, AND D

Appendix A: Practical Exercises and Tools

Exercise 1: Daily Affirmations and Visualization

Purpose: To reinforce positive beliefs and visualize goals.

Instructions:

1. Daily Affirmations:

- Write down three positive affirmations that align with your goals and values. For example: "I am confident and capable," "I attract positive opportunities," "I am dedicated to continuous growth."

- Repeat these affirmations aloud each morning and evening, focusing on the meaning and feeling behind each statement.

2. Visualization:

- Set aside 5-10 minutes each day for visualization. Find a quiet space where you can sit comfortably without distractions.

- Close your eyes and visualize your goals as if they have already been achieved. Imagine the details, emotions, and experiences associated with your success.

- Maintain a positive and confident mindset throughout the visualization process.

Exercise 2: Self-Reflection and Journaling

Purpose: To enhance self-awareness and personal growth.

Instructions:

1. Daily Journaling:

- Each evening, spend 10-15 minutes reflecting on your day. Write about your experiences, thoughts, and emotions.

- Focus on what went well, any challenges you faced, and what you learned from the day.

- Consider how your actions align with the five laws of life and identify areas for improvement.

2. Weekly Reflection:

- At the end of each week, review your journal entries. Reflect on your progress towards your goals and the lessons learned.

- Set intentions for the upcoming week based on your reflections.

Exercise 3: Empathy and Active Listening

Purpose: To foster empathy and improve communication skills.

Instructions:

1. Active Listening Practice:

- Pair up with a partner and take turns speaking and listening. When your partner speaks, focus fully on their words without interrupting.

- Reflect back what the speaker has said to confirm understanding. For example, "What I hear you saying is..."

- Discuss how active listening affects the quality of your conversation.

2. Empathy Mapping:

- Create an empathy map for someone you know. Divide a paper into four sections: Thinking, Feeling, Seeing, and Doing.

- Fill in each section with what you think the person might be experiencing in these areas based on your observations and conversations.

- Use the empathy map to guide your interactions and show greater understanding and compassion.

Exercise 4: Community Involvement and Networking

Purpose: To build and strengthen community connections.

Instructions:

1. Identify Opportunities:

- Research local organizations, events, or initiatives that align with your interests and values.

- Make a list of potential opportunities for involvement, such as volunteering, attending events, or joining groups.

2. Engage and Participate:

- Choose one or two opportunities from your list and commit to participating. Engage actively and consistently.

- Build relationships with other members by introducing yourself, sharing your interests, and offering your support.

3. Reflect on Your Experience:

- After each community involvement activity, reflect on your experience. Consider what you learned, how you felt, and the connections you made.

- Use your reflections to deepen your engagement and identify additional opportunities for contribution.

Appendix B: Recommended Reading and Resources

Books on Personal Growth and Development

1. "The 7 Habits of Highly Effective People" by Stephen R. Covey

2. "Man's Search for Meaning" by Viktor E. Frankl

3. "The Power of Now" by Eckhart Tolle

4. "Daring Greatly" by Brené Brown

5. "Mindset: The New Psychology of Success" by Carol S. Dweck

Books on Empathy and Compassion

1. "Nonviolent Communication: A Language of Life" by Marshall B. Rosenberg

2. "The Art of Empathy: A Complete Guide to Life's Most Essential Skill" by Karla McLaren

3. "Empathy: Why It Matters, and How to Get It" by Roman Krznaric

4. "The Empathy Effect: Seven Neuroscience-Based Keys for Transforming the Way We Live, Love, Work, and Connect Across Differences" by Helen Riess

Books on Community Building

1. "The Different Drum: Community Making and Peace" by M. Scott Peck

2. "Community: The Structure of Belonging" by Peter Block

3. "Bowling Alone: The Collapse and Revival of American Community" by Robert D. Putnam

Online Resources

1. Coursera: Offers online courses on personal development, mindfulness, and communication skills.

2. TED Talks: A wealth of inspirational talks on personal growth, empathy, and community building.

3. Mindfulness Apps: Apps like Headspace, Calm, and Insight Timer provide guided meditations and mindfulness exercises.

Appendix C: Goal Setting and Action Planning Templates

SMART Goals Template

Specific: What exactly do you want to achieve?
-   Goal:

____

Measurable: How will you know when you have achieved it?
-   Metrics:

____

Achievable: Is this goal realistic and attainable?

- Resources/Skills Needed:

____

Relevant: How does this goal align with your broader objectives?

- Relevance:

____

Time-Bound: What is the deadline for achieving this goal?

- Deadline:

____

Action Plan Template

Goal:

-

____

Steps to Achieve the Goal:
1.

____

2.

____

3.

____

4.

____

5.

____

Resources Needed:

-

____

Potential Obstacles and Solutions:

-

____

Progress Checkpoints:

-

____

Appendix D: Reflection and Journaling Prompts

Daily Reflection Prompts

1. What went well today? What am I grateful for?

2. What challenges did I face, and how did I handle them?

3. What did I learn today, and how can I apply it moving forward?

4. How did I demonstrate the five laws of life in my actions today?

5. What can I improve on tomorrow?

Weekly Reflection Prompts

1. What were my major accomplishments this week?

2. How did I overcome any obstacles or setbacks?

3. In what areas did I grow personally or professionally?

4. How did I contribute to my community or support others?

5. What goals will I set for the upcoming week?

By integrating these practical exercises, recommended readings, templates, and reflection prompts into your daily life, you can enhance your journey of self-discovery and growth. These tools provide a structured approach to applying the five laws of life, helping you create a life of purpose, fulfillment, and joy. Remember, the journey is ongoing, and each step forward brings you closer to your highest potential. Embrace it with curiosity, resilience, and an open heart.

www.ingramcontent.com/pod-product-compliance
Lightning Source LLC
Chambersburg PA
CBHW071245150726
48001CB00018B/135